THE OLD NEGRO
AND
THE NEW NEGRO

THE OLD NEGRO
AND
THE NEW NEGRO

by T. LeRoy Jefferson, MD

Editors

Mary M. Jefferson, MA
Mylia Tiye Mal Jaza

BePublished.Org

For Information Address:

mari@bepublished.org

THE CONGLOMERATE
P.O. Box 8324
Jackson, MS 39284

(972) 880-8316

INTRODUCTION

By
T. Le Roy Jefferson, M.D.
(1867-1939)

In attempting to write this book, I am prompted to do so to point out to my people some of the errors they are making that are holding the Negroes back as a race. I am writing this, a sort of guide for the American Negro, by pointing out some of their errors and, at the same time, suggesting some of the remedies for correcting them – trusting that they will receive and read and see the subjects discussed as I see them, and will govern themselves accordingly.

PREFACE

As this book is intended to be read by the poor readers as well as the good readers, I have tried to write it in language that the poor reader can read and understand without having a dictionary constantly at his side.

I have tried to state facts only, and in the shortest and plainest words and sentences possible, so that the readers may not only understand them but be able to remember them. For the sake of emphasis there are some things I have repeated over and over again, because of the fact that I want to deeply and indelibly impress these things on the readers' minds.

In Part I, the Old Negro is briefly portrayed to show some of the errors of the past, with the hope that it will more deeply interest the readers with the importance of the New Negro, whom I have tried to portray in Part II under the subject head of The New Negro.

In The New Negro, I have tried to portray the ideal Negro citizen in some of the more common vocations of the Negro people.

It is the request of the author that you, dear readers, read the book through before passing judgment on its merits. Then if, after having read it through, you agree with the things I have written, I ask you to dedicate the balance of your lives' actions and doings to the helping to create in the younger people of the race, the men and women of tomorrow, the ideal Negro citizen.

T. L. J.

CONTENTS

PART I – THE OLD NEGRO

PART II – THE NEW NEGRO

PART I

THE OLD NEGRO

I

The Freedmen

At the close of the war of the rebellion, the United States Government freed four million Negro slaves and then added the thirteenth and fourteenth amendments to the Constitution of the United States; thereby making them full-fledged citizens of these United States, and then and there abandoned these Negroes to their fate, grossly ignorant and penniless, to hoe their own row along beside their former educated and intelligent masters.

The results were that northern white men still chafing from the sores and antagonisms caused by the war, white men known as Carpetbaggers, came south under the guise of Republicans and preached to and converted the ignorant Negroes to the Republican Party, regardless of whether it was to the Negroes' best interests to be Republicans or Democrats; and as a result of this, where the Negroes were in the majority, they voted to elect any one to office who succeeded in getting his name on the Republican ticket – regardless as to whether such person was qualified for such office to which he aspired to be elected, or whether he would serve the best interests of all or a majority of the people, or even serve the best interest of the Negroes themselves. To those ignorant Negroes, every Republican was their friend and every Democrat was their enemy and wanted to put them back into slavery.

Thus using the poor ignorant Negroes to serve their own selfish ends and aims, Negroes just from their former masters' cotton fields were elected to such important offices as the State Legislatures and State Senates, there in gross ignorance to enact laws to govern their former masters. Just think of it, men who did not know one letter of the alphabet elected to enact laws to govern states, counties and cities, there voting to the dictates of the Carpetbaggers. And later on, the Carpetbaggers began "hogging" all of the important offices for themselves, by corralling the Negro vote under the guise of Republicanism.

During all this era, the white South was thinking of and devising means to wrest from the Negroes the control of politics and, as a result of this period of thinking and devising, there was born a white organization known as the Ku Klux Klan. This was the beginning of the ending of the Carpetbaggers' rule and of Negro domination in politics. Yet, and still after the end of the Carpetbag rule, the Negroes still held the full rights of franchise, and of course where the Negroes were in the majority, and that was practically all over the South, they still held the balance of power in the elections.

Later on, there came into being semi-organized bands of whites, known as Whitecappers and Night-Riders, which succeeded in a large measure in intimidating and scaring the Negroes away from the polls.

Yet and still, in many sections of the South, these bands were not so successful in their aims in breaking that balance of power that the Negroes held and wielded in the elections.

The white South could not disfranchise the Negro outright, being barred by the thirteenth and fourteenth amendments to the United States Constitution, which had been ratified by the states of the Union.

Southern diplomacy began to function and as a result they began adding amendments to the constitutions of the different southern states, such as the grandfather clause, which provided that for one to be eligible to vote, his grandfather would have had to have been eligible to vote. Others added a literacy clause which provided that, to be eligible to vote, one would have to be able to read or interpret any clause in the Constitution when read to him, to the satisfaction of the registration officer, thus giving to the registration officer the power to disfranchise the Negroes to a satisfactory and powerless minimum.

After years of court litigation, most of these amendments to the states' constitutions were declared unconstitutional by the Supreme Court of the United States, and by this time thousands of Negroes had lost their interest in government, politics and voting.

The most successful amendment in putting the Negroes out of politics was the poll tax clause, which provided that any one between the ages of twenty-one and fifty-five to be eligible to vote must have paid the two previous years' poll tax.

The Negro, having already lost his interest in government and voting, was just merely lukewarm on politics. There was very few who would pay two dollars just for the privilege of voting for some white candidate.

This condition grew into a situation where the politicians and monied interests that wanted to elect certain candidates would pay the Negro's poll tax for his vote, and then herd them to the polls to vote according to the politicians' dictations, regardless of the qualifications of such candidates or what they stood for. So, in this way, the Negro gradually voted himself out of politics in the South and, to be sure that he stays out, there was inaugurated the white primary, which put the Negro entirely out of politics.

II

The Republican Party in the South

The Republican Party in the South being dead except in name only, just a shell being held together by a group of keen politicians, ousted the Negro by changing to "lily white" Republicans – making just enough showing to control delegates that their states are entitled to in the national conventions, and making just enough showing to control the federal patronage in their state when we have a national Republican administration.

The Negro, after being converted to the Republican Party, looked upon every one who was a Democrat as being an enemy. Not only that, but he taught it to his children, bringing them up with hatred in their hearts for the very people who were to be his neighbors for times to come.

In the early years of freedom, during the days of Reconstruction, the Negroes were in the ascendancy in politics.

They taught their children such as would create in them a feeling of antagonism and hatred of the Southern whites. It was a common expression for them to tell their children, "If you let any white trash hit you and you don't hit them back, I will whip you." All of this was a result of the feeling created under the Carpetbag rule and influence.

They could not see or reason far enough ahead that they and the whites were destined to live here in the South as neighbors, and to try and cultivate a friendship for their neighbors rather than an antagonistic feeling of animosity against them.

After all, it has become very obvious to the right thinking Negroes that the Southern whites are their best friends – for the reason the Southern whites will open the door of opportunity for Negroes to make money and a living, although they restrict his opportunities of spending it; while the Northern whites shut the doors, in many instances, of opportunities of making money, but on the other hand offer many of the opportunities of spending his money that are restricted in the South.

So it resolves itself into this situation as regards the Southern and Northern white man: The Southern white will give the Negro his heart but not his hand, while the Northern white will give the Negro his hand but not his heart. I leave it to you, dear reader, to judge for yourself which is the Negro's best friend.

The Negro has become of no importance in the politics of the South. In some parts of the North and West, he is under leaders who are in the game for what they can get out of it for their own selfish and personal use, posing as racial leaders who influence and lead the masses of Negroes to the polls to vote for the politicians and political parties that pay the highest price. That is not helping the Negroes politically at all.

At one time, the Southern Negroes, after the end of the Carpetbag rule and before they were legislated out of politics, allowed themselves to be led to the polls by Negro leaders and voted for politicians and the Republican Party, just as is the case today with the Northern Negroes. The one difference is that they are not solidly wedded to the Republican Party as was the Southern Negro. These Negro leaders are themselves political bargain day hunters, throwing their influence where the pot boils strongest.

It is just a matter of time, unless the Northern and Western Negroes learn to support men and measures and not politicians and political parties, before the Northern Negroes will be in some way outlawed from politics as were the Southern Negroes. No race of people who allows another race of people's money to influence and control their franchise rights can survive politically forever.

It has taken years to effectually put the Negro out of politics, and it is going to take years to again put the Negro back into politics. More on that phase of the Negro in this country later on in this book.

III

U.S. Government's Error

So much better would it have been had the federal government, when it freed the Negroes, in some manner exercised some kind of a protectorate over the freedmen – and instead of giving them full franchise rights and privileges as it did, to have in some way limited the franchise and to have let the Negroes achieve the franchise gradually as they became more intellectual instead of giving full franchise rights and leaving them to be the prey and to the mercies of the Carpetbaggers posing as Republicans (and the only true friends of the freedmen), using as justification of such claims that they were Northern men and that they were Republicans. And, that it was the Northern army and The Republican party that had freed the Negroes, leaving the poor deluded freedmen to believe that the whole Northern army was a solid Republican army and that every Northern white man was a Republican and a friend of the Negroes.

Another error of the government was the freeing and giving to the Negroes the full privilege and right to go and live anywhere that pleased or suited them, without in any way warning them of the dangers of venereal diseases. It is true the government had not the knowledge of these diseases that it has now, but the Negroes should have been given such knowledge as the whites had of these diseases at that time.

As a result of this negligence on the part of the government, the young men of the country went into the towns and later on into the cities and there contracted gonorrhea and syphilis and came in contact with the tuberculosis element. And as a result, many of them became victims of these dreaded diseases, and when they became depleted of ready cash, they returned to their former homes only to spread among the innocent stay-at-homes these dreadful diseases.

This was strikingly proven during the conscription of young men for service in the World War, when such a large percent of young Negro men were found to be infected with venereal diseases. That only showed one side of the picture – the male side. Experience in private practice and in the free clinic show about an equal number of Negro women so infected.

IV

Errors of the Southern Whites

The errors that Southern whites made during the days of Reconstruction were in sitting idly by, and allowing the Carpetbaggers to come in posing as the Negroes' best friends, while they (the Southern whites) offered no gesture of friendship to the Negroes.

How different could and would have been the situation had the Southern whites intensely strived to cultivate a friendly feeling between the races and had converted the Negroes, or at least a large part of them, into the Democratic Party as did the Carpetbagger succeed in converting all of them to the Republican Party?

Then there would have been no such thing as the Negroes holding the balance of power all over the South as they did in elections. There is no reason to believe that the Southern white man with his knowledge of the Negroes could not have converted as many Negroes to the Democratic Party as did the Carpetbaggers to the Republican Party – or at least enough to have broken that balance of power the Negroes held.

Thus, by so dividing the Negro vote, there would have been no need of the Ku Klux Klan, the Whitecappers and Night-Riders, etc., to rid the South of the Carpetbagger and the domination of the Negroes in political affairs.

With the Negro votes divided and the Southern whites holding all of the important offices, there would have been no need of the many constitutional amendments that were put on the statute books of the Southern states with the sole object of disfranchising the Negroes.

All of the time and gray brain matter that were expended in formulating those amendments could have been better used in formulating plans for the development of the many resources of the South for its industrial and financial advancement.

Then, all of the people of the South, both black and white, would have been much better off and much farther advanced today industrially and financially, from an educational standpoint, and also from a point of hygiene and health.

V

The Negroes Divided

Go out today and call together the first 100 Negroes you meet, and there is no proposition that you could put before them and they would agree to 100 percent.

That was because the Negroes had not begun to think and only heard one side of the question as enunciated by the Carpetbaggers. The white South sitting idly by and not offering one gesture of friendship or advice or attempting to show the Negroes the other side of the picture.

The Carpetbaggers converted the Negroes to the Republican Party by appealing to their sense of hatred and prejudice towards their former masters. The Carpetbagger planted deeply into the Negroes' minds that any man who was a Democrat wanted to put the Negroes back into slavery and that if the Democrats succeeded in gaining control of the government that they really would put the Negroes back into slavery.

Some of the Old Negroes today still believe the white South would like to have the Negroes back into slavery. That shows just how deeply the Carpetbaggers poisoned the ex-slaves' minds against the white South. All of this was done as a matter of politics trying to perpetuate themselves in control of the Southern political situation.

VI

The Old Negro's Idea of Education

The Old Negro, when he had money to educate his children, often sent them to school and boasted to his friends and to his children that he was educating them so that they would be able to make a living and their way through this world with their heads and would not have to depend of their hands – doing manual labor for a livelihood as he himself had to do. In short, he was educating his sons for white-collar jobs.

These sons grew up with the idea in their heads that it would be a disgrace for them as educated men to do manual labor for a livelihood. And as a result with the little learning that they received, thinking that they were educated, they absolutely refused to do any kind of work that did not smack of a "white collar" job.

And rather than work for an honest living, they preyed on honest hard-working, ignorant Negro women as their sweethearts. Their little learning gave them enough business acumen to select some steady working Negro woman who had a job (most times as a cook in some wealthy family's home) so that she could feed him with "overs" from her employer's table. And she generally saw to it that there were always plenty of "overs," and of a quality that suited her lover's appetite.

This was the type of Negro who posed as racial leaders whom the politicians used to lead the ignorant Negroes to vote for politicians and political parties without regards of the ability or fitness of such candidates for holding the offices to which they aspired to be elected.

In fact, their whole argument was that any candidate who was a Republican was the Negroes' best friend, and that any candidate who was a Democrat was the Negroes' worst enemy and looked favorably on the slavery question. During all of this time, the Southern whites were studying and devising ways and means of getting the Negro menace out of the politics of the South. Just how well they succeeded: –

The Negroes' present standing in the political affairs of the South today answers that question.

VII

Booker T. Washington

To Booker T. Washington must be given the credit of dispelling from the Negroes' heads the idea or feeling that when he was educated or even partially educated that he was fitted only for a white-collar job.

For Booker T. Washington taught and proved that it was necessary for the Negroes to have some education, as much as their time and means would allow them to acquire, that they might be most successful in any line of work or labor, and in this the Southern whites heartily agreed and endorsed and encouraged him in his work at Tuskegee – hence the success of Tuskegee.

The Southern whites, being the principal employers of the masses of Negro labor in the South, soon found out that the more intelligent the Negro laborers were, the more reliable, dependable and sturdy workers they became. And they generally gave this class of Negroes the preference in their employing of laborers and by doing this they were unthinkingly laying an example to the happy-go-lucky, unreliable, shiftless kind of Negro and to the younger generation that they must mend their ways or else be shuffled out of the pack.

For it has come to the point where if two apply for the same job – one of the shiftless happy-go-lucky kind, the other of the intelligent energetic kind – the latter generally gets the job, because employers of colored help have learned from experience that the honest intelligent working Negro gives better and more dependable service than the other kind of Negro gives.

And now the influence of Tuskegee and the things that Booker T. Washington advocated and featured have spread to the Negro schools throughout the Southland. Even to the small one – and two-teacher rural schools. They are all endeavoring to give the Negro youth some form of industrial training. It is surprising to see some of the handiwork these pupils are displaying and exhibiting, when given an opportunity at the Southern county fairs. This is because industrial, as well as literal, education was advocated and taught by one who honestly had the interest in proper racial development of the Negro at heart. The teachings of Booker T. Washington have interested educators not only throughout the United States but throughout the world. Educators of many foreign countries have visited Tuskegee to see and study at first hand the methods and their effect on the Negro youth of that institution, so that they may, if found feasible, adopt those methods in the educational systems of their own countries.

So one can readily see that the influence of this new departure in Negro education as introduced and taught by Booker T. Washington has encircles the glove, interesting the leading education of the foreign nations of the world. This is because he struck upon the right chord, and, like the musician who strikes the right and harmonious chord, he attracts the attention of the listening and appreciative world.

PART II
THE NEW NEGRO

I

The New Negro—Superior to the Old Negro

The New Negro will be a much superior being to the Old Negro – physically, mentally, morally and in honesty of purposes – because of the physiological and hygienic surrounding under which he will be born and reared with the care that is being given by the local, state and federal governments (and this is just the beginning) to the unborn and growing child.

Prenatal Care

That is the attention that is being given the mother during the period of pregnancy that is the time before the child is born. The insistence and teaching are that these prospective mothers receive the very best of prenatal care so that when the child comes into this world, its advent will be under the best possible healthful and sanitary surroundings. Prospective mothers will be examined for inheritable diseases and, if found to be infected, will be treated so as to prevent the child from inheriting said diseases.

In the prenatal state, the mothers are kept in the best possible condition, circumstances being taken into consideration. For example, where a prospective mother is found to be syphilitic, she will be given the proper anti-syphilitic treatment to prevent the child being inflicted with this dreaded disease – thereby dooming the child to a low mentality, a low disease resistance, and a weakling (one who will always be behind the healthy child in development – physical, mental and moral – one always at the foot of the class, one whose weakness will have a tendency to make him easily led in the wrong direction of dishonesty, crime, lewdness and dissipation). If found to be tuberculous, all preventive measures will be employed after birth to prevent the child from being so infected. These things the governments are doing now in a limited way, but it is just a matter of time before such measures will be applied to all of the people, rural as well as town and city dwellers.

The government's efforts to reduce infant mortality, the teachings of infant care. The circulars sent out by the government health agencies. The teachings and care by the infant and pre-school nurse of the pre-school child, that is the child not yet old enough to attend school. Under these nurses, any physical defect found in a child will be referred to the family physician or to the government clinic, so that the child will be kept in its best physical condition so as to be able to advance as rapidly as is possible in the pursuance of its, studies when it reaches school age.

It is a well-recognized fact by physicians that a syphilitic person as a general rule is more careless of his or her health than others who are not syphilitics – that is, they display less self-interest in their personal health and well being, and when the disease has run on for years until their blood is just reeking with the germs of syphilis, they get in a state of don't care – and syphilitic person, as a general rule, when ill with any other disease does not respond to treatment as readily as do other non-syphilitics. I have often come in contact with syphilitics who were provided with ample means to take treatment to cure themselves and, when advised of the need of taking ample treatment to cure themselves, absolutely refused to take any treatment at all – preferring to go on in their idle, shiftless and slothful way.

Think of the New Negro who has been taught of this dreadful disease and what a different being he will be from the Old Negro. He will consult his physician periodically for health examinations, and then will obey the doctor's orders – a healthy human being.

The day is not far distant when tuberculous parents will not be allowed the rearing of their offspring or the mingling with the public. A tuberculous person will be compelled to go to a tuberculosis sanitarium.

It was at one time believed that children of tuberculous parents inherited the disease, but science has amply disproved this theory and belief.

But where a child is reared by tuberculous parents, the child being brought up in a tuberculous surrounding, such a child nearly always becomes infected with tuberculosis, which if it survives in infancy and childhood nearly always succumbs to it in later years – hence the heroic efforts being put forth by the governments (local, state and national) to curb this ravage and lower the death rate from tuberculosis.

We may expect in the near future health rules and regulations discouraging and forbidding tuberculous parents rearing their own children. These health organizations will, with the aid of the government, send these children of tuberculous parents to non-tuberculous nurseries or other non-tuberculous surroundings where a check will be kept on them to show any abnormal or unnatural development which will be promptly reported to the physician in charge of such work.

A check will be kept on the growth and development to show any underweight, underdevelopment or anything resulting from undernourishment or other causes which, under the directions of the physician, will be corrected, or any defect in the teeth will be remedied by the dentist.

When these children reach the school age, under the watchful care of the school nurse and physician, tonsils and adenoids or any other maldevelopments will be carefully watched and checked, and their removal or treatment will be recommended and referred to the family physician or the government clinics.

The prevention of such diseases as smallpox, diphtheria and typhoid fever will result from giving these children the proper vaccines and serums. All in all, they will be kept in the best possible healthy conditions conducing to the best possible conditions for study and advancement.

The older Negroes are fast becoming reconciled to the use and needs of vaccines and other preventive measures used in the fight on preventable diseases.

Years ago, parents of at least 60% of the Negro children could not be persuaded to have their children vaccinated and inoculated against these diseases.

Ah, how different now. When a free clinic for the administration of these preventive measures is opened to the school children, fully 95% of the parents readily agree for their children to be so treated. In fact, it is just a matter of a very few short years, before the health authorities will require that every child to be accepted in the public schools as a pupil will have to be vaccinated and inoculated against such diseases as smallpox, typhoid and diphtheria – not only in the city and larger town schools, but in all the public schools, rural as well as town and city schools.

When these children grow older and after reaching the age of adolescence, that is growing from the state of childhood to man and womanhood (the years of the teens), they will continue to receive the same hygienic care and will, in addition, be taught in plain language the dangers of venereal diseases.

It was in the not far part considered that a person who would openly and publicly speak of venereal diseases and their dangers and consequences, such as gonorrhea and syphilis, was a vulgar person and was not considered as a proper person to address the public.

Thanks to common sense that is beginning to prevail, this mask of false modesty is being thrown off and the bare unmasked facts about the results of venereal diseases are being told to the people and especially those in the adolescent stage, as it is a well-known fact that they will ultimately learn of these diseases and, in many cases, to their sorrow then it is too late. These youngsters will be shown stereopticon views of the results of these diseases, also museum specimens will be exhibited to them, to act as a deterrent – making them stop and think twice, yes even thrice, before starting the "sowing of wild oats."

It was in consideration of all the above mentioned facts that the assertion was made that the New Negro will be a much superior being to the Old Negro – physically, mentally and morally, as well as his honesty of purposes.

II

The New Negro in Service

The Negro race being a dependent race, the Negro must, of necessity in the majority of the race, look for an employment in service.

This being realized by the New Negro, will make him different from the Old Negro in many respects.

The New Negro will be ambitious and with a craving to have and to do something, and acknowledging that the realization of these things will depend entirely upon his own efforts.

He will be, first of all things, honest and industrious, and with a determination to have something by the saving of his earnings. These factors will make of him a real trustworthy being.

And as a consequence of this, when employed on a job, his employer will know that he can rely upon him in whatever he is employed to do – as he will find the New Negro to be honest, industrious and trustworthy in every way.

The New Negro servant will not, just so soon as he accumulates a few dollars ahead, come to his employer with the excuse his father, mother, brother, sister or some other near relative is either very sick and not expected to live or else is dead, and that he must go and see them before they die or else go to the funeral of some one already dead. All this to get off the job to go away and spend the few dollars that he has accumulated.

Money will not burn the New Negro's pocket as it does the Old Negro's pocket, thus creating a burning desire to get out and spend it as a "show off."

The average Old Negro, if he succeeds in saving $100 ahead, becomes a very restless being and cannot be kept on the job until he has had a vacation long enough to have spent it, a few days or weeks, just according to the ideas and whims of the possessor. When his money is gone and he becomes hungry, he becomes a very humble and obedient person, willing to work at anything that will give him means to provide food. In many instances, he will accept a job of much smaller pay than the one that he, just a few weeks past, has abandoned – in lots of instances, without giving his employer any advance notice and time to get someone else to fill his place.

Another class of the Old Negro will work and save until he has accumulated a few hundred dollars, and then instead of putting it into a home or some other useful purpose, will put it in an automobile of far more expensive costs than his wages justify.

The desires and yearnings to own an automobile to "keep up with the Joneses" is today the reason that hundreds of thousands of families, both white and black so far as that goes, are renters instead of homeowners. Just so soon as the Old Negro comes in possession of this fine new car, he becomes helpless for walking even to his work, which he has always done before.

He will drive his new car to his work and then park it for the day in front of his employer's residence or place of business, as the case may be.

Oft, very often, he will buy a car that is better than that of his employer, to be parked all day prominently in the foreground of his employer's premises or place of business as a decoration.

His common sense of reasoning, if he has any, ought to bring him to the conclusion that his employer did not employ him as a decorator of the front of his premises or place of business as the case may be.

Naturally his employer's friends compliment him on the appearance of his new car, which will only serve to embarrass his employer, who is compelled to admit that it is not his car but that it is the property of his hired man – which brings the thought and often the remark that his Negro servant has a better car than his boss.

And very soon for some frivolous reason, and in many instances no reason at all, Mr. Negro is told that his services are no longer needed.

The New Negro servant, of course, when he really needs a car will get one; but he will use the good judgment to get one at a price that is in the range of his ability to pay for, and he will not let it have the effect of paralyzing him from walking to his work. He will use his car when he really needs to use it.

The New Negro will be quite different from the Old Negro. He will be a lover of money and will always have some important object to accomplish with his money and savings.

It will be quite necessary for him to do this to keep abreast of the other New Negroes who will be progressive and saving, and always striving to accomplish some worthy aims. Hence, we will not, as is the custom with the Old Negro, see the New Negro going to work on Monday morning "broke" and frequently in debt, when fortunate enough to find someone who will extend him credit.

The New Negro will, when he receives his pay at the end of the week, first pay those whom he owes, especially his board, lodging, grocery bill, etc., as the case may be. This is because of the training and rearing given the New Negro under this new era of things as taught by the New Negro school teacher and preached to him by the New Negro preacher, together with the home training he will have received at the hands of the New Negro parents and the New Negro surroundings everywhere.

The combination of all these factors will tend to develop in the New Negro youth ambitious aspirations to higher ideals; thereby making of the New Negro in service a more honest and dependable worker. And then and not until then will the Negroes be able to regain and hold their positions in service and not be rooted out by white foreign laborers. As a general rule, Southern white employers prefer good, honest, industrious colored service to some of the Caucasian service they make out with because of the fact that the Old Negro service has so often proven to be unreliable, untrustworthy and oftentimes dishonest and roguish.

The New Negro being strictly honest will not, if he feels or thinks that he is not receiving just or ample pay for his services, endeavor to make it up by pilfering the property of his employer and peddling it out at night to such persons who are willing to buy "hot stuff" at bargain prices as has been and still is the case today with lots of the Old Negroes in service.

If the New Negro feels that he is not receiving just and fair wages for his service, he will seek to find employment where he feels that the payment is just and fair for the services rendered. He will not attempt to make up any deficiency that he feels is lacking in the pay he receives for his services by pilfering and selling that which is not his own.

The New Negro chauffeur will not, when his day's work is finished and he is told to put his employer's car in the garage for the night, take his employer's car and spend half the night joy riding and burning up fuel at his employer's expense. He will realize that at such times more accidents will happen to the car than at other times when in the service of his employer, and too he will realize that if he, after driving the car all day for his employer, spends half the night joy riding that he will not be as well fitted for work the next day as he would have been if he had taken a full night's rest.

When this New Negro comes upon the arena of action, we will witness the New Negro getting back some of the many jobs that were once looked upon as Negro jobs, that have slipped from the Old Negro and are now being filled by Caucasian laborers in all the fields of service and labor.

This is because the Southern whites naturally prefer proficient and dependable colored service to some of the white service that they are putting up with in preference to shiftless, undependable colored labor that some of the Old Negroes give.

The New Negro, having been brought up in healthy and hygienic surroundings and having been taught the fundamental principles of hygiene and health, will practice these things – and especially that of keeping his or her body clean and will not go into service with the odors of perspiration, etc., emanating from their bodies to the disgust and displeasure of others.

The New Negro, when his day's work is finished, will go home, have a bath and change his or her working clothes for others suited to going out in company of others. Then one can go to any gathering, church, theatre, dance or other gathering without going there with a dread of the various odors that usually greet the olfactory nerves at such gatherings of the Old Negroes.

The New Negro, by observing the laws of hygiene, will be healthier and as a result will lose less time from his or her work on account of illness.

III

The New Negro in the Professions

The New Negro in the professional field will especially show the beneficial results of the good breeding and rearing under the guidance of the different public health units of governments (national, state, county, city and local) which will continue to be more powerful for the good of all of the people as time moves along.

Because those in authority are well aware of the fact that it is an impossibility for two races of people to live intermixed as are the Caucasians and Negroes of the South, and one of the races to be kept healthy under the laws of sanitation and hygiene to the total neglect of the other race.

Those in authority are realizing more and more every day that more strenuous efforts to carry out the laws of hygiene and sanitation among all of the people are becoming more and more evident every day. Owing to the Negroes' financial circumstances these measures of health improvement and sanitation are as much or more needed among the Negroes than among the whites.

If a contagious disease develops in the most squalid Negro quarters of a town or city, there will be residing in those quarters some Negro servant of some of the best, well-regulated and sanitary households of the whites of such town or city.

Hence, we may expect and will see, in the future, more attention being given sanitation and hygienic conditions in the congested and squalid Negro districts; and all of this will tend to produce a healthier and physiologically stronger type of Negro manhood and womanhood. This will, of course, produce a higher grade of individuals who will enter the professions as a life's vocation – men and women with higher ideals than are many of those now in the professional fields. Men and women with honesty of aims and purposes of doing more for their people than just getting all of the money they can, as are doing lots of those who are in the professional fields today.

I do not want to be understood as intimating that these New Negro professionals will lose sight of the honest money that they earn, for they will be strictly businessmen and business women, and of course will strictly see after and attend to the financial side of their affairs. It will be necessary for them to do this to be able to achieve other objectives. But I do mean that the New Negro professional will not take a mean advantage over the other less enlightened and short seeing Negroes to mulct them out of their hard earned dollars. These New Negro professionals will be people who will be leaders of the people in civic and other affairs that will redound to racial betterment.

The New Negro professionals will proceed with logic and reason in their work among the Negro people, thereby avoiding excitement, bombast and self-aggrandizement, as are many of those in the professions doing today.

The New Negro lawyer will not advise people to go into lawsuits that he, the lawyer, well knows that they have no chance of ever winning, just for the sake of the fee he will get out of it for fighting the case.

Nor will the dentist encourage the putting in of a lot of gold teeth to replace other teeth that could be saved just for the sake of the dollars that he gets for doing the job. Nor will the New Negro dentist advise treatment to save a tooth that he too well knows ought to be extracted – keeping alive the "goose that is laying the golden egg."

The New Negro doctor will not always, when he finds a patient with money and a willingness to pay, discover some serious ailment that it is going to take a long period of time to cure and that it will require his constant and regular care for such patient to ever get well. Neither will the New Negro doctor, when he finds a patient with money to be suffering with some incurable disease, encourage and make him believe that he can cure him until he gets all of the patient's available cash, finds that the patient's health has further deteriorated, then recommends that the patient go to some free clinic or sanitarium.

The New Negro professional, being of high moral character and well educated in heart and hand – as well as in the head, and having the best interests of his people at heart – will not stoop to such practices, as above mentioned, but will be honest and just in his dealings with his fellow man, be he rich or poor, high or low.

I am writing this because I have known of countless instances where the so-called educated Negroes, sometimes professionals educated in the head only, would seek out some ignorant Negro who had been fortunate by thrift, inheritance or other means to have amasses or in some way come into a considerable amount of ready cash. And this so-called educated Negro would seek such persons out with some great fantastic proposition in order to get his hands upon the cash of such an ignorant Negro, with no thought or intent of ever paying it back.

The New Negro, being educated in his hands and heart as well as in his head, will not stoop to such practices. He will be a reader and a believer in the Bible, and he will believe and know that whatsoever a man sows the same shall he or his descendants reap again, and I say with interest, because the Holy Scriptures tell us very plainly that "The iniquities of the parents shall fall upon the children even unto the third and fourth generations."

As a proof of this, one only has to think back and readily can recall many and many instances of people who were once good livers and were apparently prosperous on ill gotten gains, only to remember these same people dying in poverty, misery, want and shame.

The New Negro, seeing and knowing of such instances, will choose to travel the path of the honest, the upright and the just. When the number of New Negroes, or rather the number of Negroes who will conform to the New Negro ideas, come in the majority of all the Negro people, then and not until then will the Negro race become one of the chosen races of the earth.

Of course this will take years and lots of work on the part of the right thinking Negroes, just as it as taken years for the Negro to be brought down to political and other insignificances.

It is my plea in this book to my people to utilize all of the advantages that the government is offering to the Negroes in the ways of health, hygiene and education, encouraging the young Negroes to grasp these different opportunities that are being offered for their improvement. It is upon us as parents to so urge them – for it is upon them and their children that the advancement of the work of creating or bringing into being this New Negro rests. As the times pass, those with the Old Negro ideas in their heads shall find it becomes easier to pass on the work of creating this New Negro.

The New Negro professionals will not be of the type of some of the present day professionals who, because of the fact that they were the first to enter the work of their calling in a certain town or locality, think that territory is exclusively their own. And it is that they owe it to themselves to forget professional ethics and proceed to fight any one else of the same profession who may choose to locate there. The New Negro's education and knowledge of the ethics of his profession will forbid him stooping to such methods. The New Negro will not, if one happens to be a Methodist and the other a Baptist, in a few months have the town divided into two camps fighting for the professional of their respective denominations. On the contrary, the New Negro professionals will work hand in hand together, and if differences should arise between them, they will settle it between themselves and not take it to the public for the public decision of such differences.

The newcomer will not come in, in a fighting and criticizing mood because of the fact that he, fresh from school with (as he thinks) all of the latest methods of procedure in the practice of his chosen profession, forgetting the experience that the older professional has to pit against his new and untried methods. Professional cooperation will be the watchword of the New Negro professionals.

IV

The New Negro in Business

In the business world is where the New Negro will especially show his superiority over the Old Negro.

The New Negro will first post himself on business methods and principles, before venturing into business. He will not – as has been the custom with the Old Negro, just because he had enough money to buy a stock of goods – venture into business without considering any of the many angles of business that needed to be well pondered, in order to be able to open a business that would prove successful and profitable.

The New Negro will consider well all angles of business, such as rent, overhead, location of the business, the temperament of those whom he contemplates as patrons and supporters of his business, and also the appearance of the quarters in which he expects to do business.

Rent: Will the contemplated business afford sufficient revenue over other expenses to pay rent and leave a balance sufficient to meet other expenses and net the owner a profit? Even though he may own the premises in which he contemplates opening the business, he should pay himself a rental equal to what he would charge another person for the rent of the same premises.

Overhead: These expenses will be considered from every angle to determine the best ways and means of cutting it to a minimum. In the overhead expenses, he will calculate a reasonable wage for his own services and time given to the business.

Location: This is the most important business aspect of all. I will say here that one of the most grievous mistakes of the Old Negro business people was the idea of isolation of the location of his business. He was possessed with the idea that, if he could or should locate his place of business in some locality of the town or city that was well and thickly populated and at the same time some considerable distance from any other business of the same kind, he could "hog" or control the business of that locality in his line of business – only to find out later, to his sorrow, that the only way to do that was to do a general credit business to everybody. And that soon broke him.

The New Negro, having studied the principles and fundamentals of business, will readily know that the concentration of business to one locality will mean better access, more cash trade, and more and better success for the business.

The more concentrated are the different or even the same kind of businesses, the more will the people congregate in that district or locality to do their shopping. Why? Because they will know that if they cannot find what they want in one place of business, they can find it in another place only a few doors away or at most a block away. They will not be compelled to go to the other side of town to secure what they want in order to be able to give their trade to a colored merchant located in some isolated section of the town or city, and they maybe not find it there. Rather than take such chances, they will go into the white business district where they can get all of their needs met within one or two blocks.

The new Negro business people will perceive that not only will the town and city dwellers flock to the concentrated business districts, but that the country people – that great farming element which forms such a strong link in the chain of retail business in the towns and smaller cities – will, when they come in to do their shopping, head directly to the concentrated business districts where they can do their window shopping and also their real shopping.

The Old Negro, when he opened a business, the day he opened it, his establishment presented its best appearance. From that day onward, the appearance of his establishment became less and less attractive.

For example, let's say the Old Negro opened a restaurant or eating place. One would find new chinaware, new silverware, new cooking utensils, new tablecloths and napkins. Thus fitted out, he would do a good business for a while. Six or eight months later, if you should go into his place of business, you would find the same old arrangement of things, all showing the effect of wear and neglect – oilcloth table covers worn through to the wood of the table, dishes and plates nicked and cracked, the same old curtains to the windows, and other decorations that he used in his grand opening still doing service.

Should you inquire of him how his business was doing, he would inform you that business was no good, that the people do not appreciate a colored business. He would also tell you that the people patronized him well when he first opened up, but that their patronage was not permanent and that they are always looking for something new.

Mind you, right there in that last sentence, he has diagnosed the whole reason of his loss of business. If he was able to discover that they were looking for something new, then why could he not reason that to hold the people's trade it was necessary for him to keep his place presenting a new appearance – not solely by always buying new things for his business, but by the proper arrangement and rearrangement of the things he already had. Thus, giving his place of business a new appearance at least once every month.

Lots of times, by simply moving a showcase and changing and rearranging its contents, the place of business would have been given a new appearance. In fact, that is the secret of the success of many businessmen, keeping the arrangement of their stock and their places presenting a new appearance.

Another thing the New Negro businessman will not do is, when he finds himself in a successful business and making money, get the idea in his head that he is well fixed and that he must show the world that he is a big and successful businessman. He will not proceed to buy the finest car in his community and then take regular and long trips away, displaying himself and family to the world as big rich people. Nor will he attempt to build for himself and family the finest house in town.

His common sense will tell him that when he starts cutting such capers, that some one will start figuring on his downfall, which will sooner or later come. The successful New Negro businessman will save and invest his surplus cash to the best advantages, with the idea of when old age overtakes him he can retire with enough to care for himself and family the balance of his days.

He will do these things because he will know from the past history of the Negro businessmen that they got the idea in their heads too early that they were rich, when they had only reached a successful stage in their business that just put them in a position to accumulate some money for use in their older days.

The Old Negro, if he went into business and was fortunate to get $1,000 ahead, got the idea in his head that he was rich; and then he paid more attention to spending than he did to saving, which soon brought him, only too late, to a realization of his error. For nine times out of 10, he was never able to recoup the business that he let slip from his command during the days of his "riches."

The New Negro businessman or woman will be a strictly business person, using the head and pencil and keeping up with all angles of the business – keeping the books on a strictly business basis with a keen eye for detecting leaks.

He or she will be able, at a glance through the books and the business, to know which departments are paying and how much; and which departments are not paying and how much they are losing, thereby being in a position to put such departments that are not paying on a paying basis or either eliminating them.

So many of the Old Negro business people have held on to some department of their business that was not a paying proposition until it sapped all the life and profit out of the departments that were paying propositions, and were not able to tell or know why their business was failing. All of this was due to the fact that they had no system to their business.

It is true, the New Negro business people will come in direct competition with the foreigner who has just about rooted the business Negroes out of every business that depends almost solely upon Negro trade for its principal support, with the exception of the Negro barbershop. All over the South at one time, certain businesses that were looked upon as belonging to the Negroes are, at this time, almost totally absorbed by the foreigners.

The New Negro business people, with the backing of the New Negroes, will set out to recoup that business, first of all by giving to their people, in every way, better service and more clean and attractive places of business, better accommodations, higher quality of products, and, in fact, better in every way and just as reasonable prices as Mr. Foreigner will be giving.

And when the New Negro does these things and the New Negro ideas continue to be developed in the younger Negroes, the men and women of tomorrow, he will realize that he will gradually recoup the Negro trade that the Old Negro business people let slip from them – owing it to the bad management, bad treatment and poor service they gave to their people.

The Old Negro had an idea that just because he was colored, that by being so, was all that he needed to hold the Negro trade, regardless of the kind of service or products he offered to his people. The New Negro business people will be supported by the New Negroes, who will be constantly increasing in all the different vocations of life and spreading the New Negro ideas among the people, while we of the old school will be constantly dying and lessening in number – and may God hasten that day as lots of us old Negroes with our old fossil ideas are merely cogs in the wheels of racial progress and advancement.

There are lots of the old idea Negroes who really believe that what a white merchant offers for sale is really superior to that offered by the Negro merchant, although offered at the same price and made by the same manufacturer. That, in some instances, can be accounted for in the differences in appearance between the Caucasian store and the Old Negro store.

But, as I have already pointed out in this chapter, the New Negro merchant will keep his place of business up-to-date, not only in appearance, but also in the quality of the products he offers for sale and consumption. And, especially will he give his people up-too-date and as courteous service as it to be had in any other store, be it white, colored or foreigner.

The New Negro business people, as well as others who are fortunate in saving some money, will educate their children but not in a haphazard way as has been, and is being, done by a great many of our people. When there is doubt as to the best line of education suited to a child, that child will be sent to a vocational guidance school that is provided by the government, and let it be determined the best line of education suited to that child.

Then the parents will spend their money in educating that child along the lines pointed out by such schools. They will not, when a child finishes high school, push him right on through college and a professional course of what they want their child to be when the child's natural trend was to a mechanical, agricultural or some other line of work.

V

The New Negro School Teacher

First of all, the New Negro school teachers will be fully qualified citizens in every way, and also will be fully qualified in the teaching art.

The New Negro teachers will stay qualified as citizens, teachers and leaders by constant study not only at home, but will be active members and regular attendants of their local and state teachers' associations. And will, whenever possible, attend the National Teachers Association and be participants in local and state civic affairs, and will also subscribe for and read at least one educational journal of national importance.

These new teachers will attend some summer school for teachers every year possible, thereby keeping abreast of all the latest methods known to the teaching art.

They will readily appreciate the fact that, in order to be able to give to those under their tutelage that which will make for the best in their advancement thereby making for the best in racial advancement will need teachers with a combination of all of the above named factors.

The New Negro teachers will not be teachers by rote centering their activities on teaching the three Rs, "Reading, 'Riting and 'Rithmetic" as did the Old Negro teachers. The new teachers will be practical in their work, teaching everything that will be of practical usage to their pupils in after life.

They will teach and impress upon their pupils the importance of obeying and respecting their superiors and seniors, and of respecting and obeying the laws of the land and health – such as the importance of taking regular periodical health examinations, which will not only consist of periodical medical examinations, but regular dental examinations as well. They will teach them the importance of self-sacrifices and the needs of being regular in their habits (good habits) and of being honest in their dealings with their fellow man.

These new teachers will fully realize that for persons to be truly educated, that such persons must be educated not only in the head by the mastery of books, but must also be educated in their hands by being willing, able and ready to do whatever they will that their hands may find to do in the struggle of life. They must also be educated in their hearts, which will act as a governor of their actions and doings – that inward determination of right that will guide them in their daily dealings with their fellow man.

Dealing with them as they themselves would like to be dealt with were they in their fellow man's place and their fellow man was in their place. Until a person is so educated, he is not properly educated but only partially educated with only one or two of the principal factors of education. Such education has proven dangerous, and in countless instances, even disastrous to many of the so-styled old educated Negroes. These New Negro teachers, realizing these defects, will exert their energies and efforts to wholly educating those who may come under them as students.

In fact, the whole trend of Negro education should and must be based on the ideas promulgated by the late and lamented Booker T. Washington. Give them this kind of an education and they will go out into the world prepared and determined to do whatever their hands find to do, whether it be manual labor, white collar jobs or professional work.

There is something radically wrong with the whole Negro education system in this country. Of the tens of thousands of young men and women who graduate from the high schools and colleges in this country every year, not 2% of them graduate with the ideas of the importance of qualified citizenship instilled in their minds − when in fact, when they graduate from high school or college, they should have had the ideas and principles of good citizenship so drilled into them that they would ever feel it a civic disgrace after reaching the age of 21 to not be and ever remain a qualified citizen.

To you Mr., Mrs., and Miss School Teacher, I will say that the government is paying you as teachers to make of the men and women of tomorrow better citizens than are the men and women of today. If you are not working to the accomplishment of this aim of the government, you are not honestly earning the salary, though small it may be, that the government is paying you.

During the later years, the schools are stressing athletics as a part of their program. That is all right in its place in making for physically healthier and stronger individuals. Overall, I hold it is wrong and you are doing the children an injustice in giving all extra times and efforts to the development of athletes at the expense of good citizenship. I will ask you in all fairness: Which is of more importance and benefit to the race in its advancement − an athlete or full-fledged citizen? The New Negro school teacher will be a fully qualified citizen.

I truly hope the day is not far distant when it will be one of the government's requirements of all teachers that they must be fully qualified citizens. Then, a teacher can stand up before a class of students and talk citizenship, its principles, needs and the importance of every one being qualified as a citizen. They can talk and teach it with a clear conscience. The teachers of today cannot do that for fear that some inquisitive child might inquire of them if they are fully qualified as citizens. Many of the present day teachers cannot tell what constitutes a full-fledged citizen.

Can we then be surprised that the younger Negroes have no interest in citizenship and government?

There are lots of counties in some parts of the South where it would be impossible to impanel or summon a panel of 25 Negroes who were fully qualified as citizens to serve the state as jurors.

The teaching of the principles of citizenship, and the need of their being and keeping themselves qualified as citizens, will be one of the principal duties that the New Negro school teachers will feel they are obligated to fulfill. They will continually keep to the front in the classroom, and in the minds of their pupils, the subject of good citizenship. When these pupils, the men and women of tomorrow and their children, grow into man and womanhood, they will see things in a different light to what the Old Negro saw it and to this day still sees it – that the only thing that one needed to keep qualified for was to be able to vote at election time. Thus enabling some few Negro leaders to exploit and barter their votes for what cash they could get out of the politicians for using their influence to throw the Negro vote a certain way, which eventually threw the Negro vote entirely out of politics in the South.

The New Negro school teacher will well know that voting is just one of the subsidiary reasons why the Negroes should be and stay qualified as full-fledged citizens.

There being other important reasons also (as example, serving on juries, as coroner, for civil or criminal) and being eligible to fill any appointive office in the government, being eligible to participate in any donations or doles of the government, and for serving as administrators of estates.

Now, in regard to government donations or doles: During the late depressing when government money was appropriated for the relief of its starving and needy citizens by providing work for those in need and want, there came from many places complaints that the Caucasians were being provided first and then what was left went to the Negroes.

Did you ever stop and look the matter square in the face? That these provisions were made by the government with a view to relieving its citizens of hunger and want – and that the masses of the Negroes in this country are not full-fledged citizens of this United States

Government because they are not qualified citizens of the cities, counties and states in which they live. They are just living here or are naturalized residents or naturalized wards of the United States Government. Those in charge of the distribution of the relief work naturally looked out for the needy citizens first, and the nation's wards and residents later.

As administrators of estates, let us suppose that some Negro who was worth a considerable amount in property and money should, in his will, designate some colored person to be administrator of his estate but the probate judge should want to make some white person the administrator. The judge could disqualify the Negro on the ground that he was not a qualified citizen, and appoint some white person. All of the courts in the land would uphold and endorse the probate judge's actions in his so doing.

So one can readily see that there are other just as important reasons for keeping oneself qualified as a full-fledged citizen, and being able to vote at election time.

The New Negro teachers, being fully aware of these conditions and knowing the needs of their being remedied, will so hammer and instill into the very beings of their pupils the principles and needs of good citizenship that they will, ever after reaching their majority, qualify themselves and ever remain good citizens – thereby making themselves a part of this good old Democratic form of government of ours, being ever ready for any call of their government. When one is fully qualified as a citizen of his government, he is not simply living under the protection of that government but is himself a part of his government. For a government is made up of the citizens of the government, and not of the residents of the government.

The Old Negro has just about lost all claims on the government with the exception of being a resident of the governmental territory and in a small way a property owner. Simply owning property does not constitute full-fledged citizenship if the owner is lax and remiss in fully discharging other governmental obligations and requirements imposed upon the citizens of that government.

All of these things, the New Negro teacher will teach and drill into the heads of their pupils. These things to these new teachers will be as important a duty as teaching the three Rs, athletics, etc., which are often carried to the extreme by the present day Negro school teachers at the expense and neglect of other things that would prove far more useful to the young Negro graduate in his or her work in after life.

I do not want to be understood as opposing athletics. On the contrary, I heartily endorse athletics for the young people, but not at the expense and neglect of other more important attainments of the rounded out educational factors that will be helpful to the student in after years in life's struggle.

Now, as a last plea to you Mr., Mrs., and Miss School Teacher, I implore you to qualify yourselves as full-fledged citizens. That will enable you to, with a clear conscience, stand up before your scholars and impart to them and impress upon their minds the needs of the Negroes being and remaining fully qualified citizens. And when you shall have done this, you not only will be honestly earning the salary that the government is paying you, but will be introducing into the Negro educational system one of the best principles that has been introduced in the Negro educational system since the late Booker T. Washington advocated and introduced the idea of industrial Negro education.

VI

The New Negro—His Children and Their Education

The tendency of the present day Negro parents, especially in recent years, seems to be to center their energies on educating their girls to the almost total neglect of their boys. I have studied the catalogues of several race schools and find that the percentage of girl students, especially in the advanced grades, to exceed by a very large percentage that of boy students. Just the contrary of what should be.

Can we as a race hope to take our rightful place among the other races of this world through the efforts and endeavors of our women? Are we trying to set up a precedence in Negro education by educating our girls to the almost total neglect of the education of our boys?

In all history, I have ever read – both sacred and profane, ancient, medieval and modern of all the races that have made any history worthy of record – that history has been made by the men of such races; and in none of the races do we find where the preference in educational development has been or is being given to the women save in the American Negro race, and more particularly in recent years.

Let us take a brief glance over ancient history – first sacred.

When the Lord decreed to people this world, He first made man and then later He created woman, we are told, as a help-mate and company keeper of man.

And as we trace sacred history through the years, and centuries, we find that when He wanted someone to lead His chosen people out of Egyptian bondage, He raised up among them a man to so lead them – Moses. And right along through the ages of the Old Testament of the time of the coming of Christ, we find that all of the successful prophets, kings and rulers of the people were men, and when the Almighty was ready to send a redeemer of the world, He sent His son – not his daughter.

In all profane history, from the very dawn of intellectual development and advancement, we find that all of the leaders of those races that lead in the advancement of literature, science, music, medicine, law and the fine arts to have been the men of such races and so on down to the present day. The greatest leaders, diplomats and statesmen of the leading nations of the world today are men of such nations.

I want to deeply impress on your minds, dear readers, that if the Negro race of America is ever to take its rightful place in the civic, political, industrial, intellectual, and financial affairs of America, we must raise up and educate men. Men of ability, men who will with their tireless energy – their indomitable courage, their forceful eloquence, and their logical diplomacy – go into the halls of Congress, into the state legislatures, before the courts of the land, and out into the world at large and plead the cause of the Negro people.

I once visited a Baptist association that was being held in a small town situation in a thickly populated farming section largely inhabited by colored people.

The town, being incorporated, had no mayor or other town official to deliver the address of welcome on behalf of the town. But it so happened that one of the county commissioners, who has a Baptist deacon, lived in the town and, of course, he was invited to deliver the welcome address on behalf of the town. Contrary to the usual custom, the local program was so arranged that his address of welcome was the last number on the program.

He began his address by expressing his great surprise to learn that the little town had the local talent to render such an elegantly beautiful and intellectual program as had just been rendered.

He also expressed greater surprise at their not having one of the local boys on the program. Then, as though afraid that he would say something to start someone thinking, he stopped very abruptly and began speaking of something else.

In speaking on economy, he told of the large amount of money that was paid out there during the harvesting season, and said that he had often wondered where and for what purpose that money was being spent.

Making himself interested, he said that he made inquiries at the different local stores, only to find that a very small percentage was being spent there; but that inquiries made at the local post office and express office revealed the fact that a very large percentage of it was being sent away to the mail order houses for silk shirts, socks and neckties, Norfolk suits, Stetson hats, tooth picks, shoes, etc.

The moderator, by way of replying, deplored and dilated on the fact that the young men were spending the greater part of their earnings for fine clothes.

I have always had a hesitancy to speaking in public, but that was one time that I wanted the opportunity to tell that moderator and that audience that why those boys and young men were spending the greater part of their earnings for fine clothes was to try and make themselves look handsome and attractive to those girls when they came home from college, as they had been so neglected in their education that they had nothing within their heads with which to attract and entertain them. I also wanted to tell them that what he was saying was not a reflection on those boys and young men, but was a reflection on us grown ups for not having done our duty to those boys.

In conversation with one of the leading ministers in the African Methodist Episcopal Church, I was told they were really up a tree when it came to supplying some of their churches with intelligently qualified ministers – as they had lots of churches where the intelligence of the congregations was far superior to that of such ministers as the church had with which to supply them. He was lamenting the fact that such few, practically none, of the intelligent young men took to the ministry.

I told him that the fault lies within the church itself, and as an example, I told him of visiting one of their Sunday School conventions that had more than 100 young people in attendance as delegates, and, when I was introduced to the convention, I inquired how many of its delegates were boys and was informed that there were only five.

Just think of that, only five – when the majority of that delegation of young people ought to have been boys.

They ought to have been there reading papers, working on committees, saying speeches and doing such other things as would accustom them to appearing before the public and audiences. This being done, the task of supplying intelligent ministers would become much easier. I also told him of my having visited a Sunday School just a few Sundays previous, and counted 45 girls and only 15 boys as present, and these boys, with the exception of five, were under the age of 10 – were tots. And on leaving Sunday School and driving through the streets, I counted nearly 100 boys under the age of 20 loafing on the streets, lounging around boot-black stands, and moving picture places, garages and playing in the streets and alleys. I told him that right there on the streets and alleys was the material for his intelligent preachers and leaders going to waste before our eyes.

Boys of some of our best families and residents who seem to have lost all interest in the intelligent rearing of their sons, upon whom the continued advancement and development of the American Negro almost wholly depends, are seldom found in leading positions.

There were some factors that led up to this state of affairs of neglecting the boys' education. One I will speak of in particular is the resulting high wages incident to the World War, making it possible for a mere boy to earn greater wages than men earned before the War.

This was one of the alluring temptations to keep the boys out of school. Parents who, in their greed for worldly goods, sacrificed the education of their boys for the almighty dollar. And as a justification and excuse, they offered such fallacious arguments as: that if you educated too many boys there would be no jobs for them and that they would not want to do common labor, and would become, as it were, a drug on the market and it would be money wasted on their education.

I want to tell you right here to have no fear for the boy or young man who is properly educated in heart, hand and head not finding a job – for if he finds no job awaiting him, he will get out into the world and make a job for himself. The old argument that if you educate too many men that there will be nothing for them to do is one of the weakest ever.

In the State of Georgia, there is just one Negro physician to more than every 20,000 Negroes, when one physician is supposed to be able to properly care for only 1,000 people. Just see what a vast field exists in this one vocation for the properly educated Negro? In dentistry, we have larger proportions. In law, the percentage is tripled to what it is in medicine and dentistry.

I merely spoke of Georgia as one example. The ratio in other Southern states in some instances are just as large or larger, in others it is smaller. But taking all as a whole, one can see what a vast field awaits tens of thousands properly educated Negro boys and young men in the professional world alone.

When you hear parents making such excuses as there would be nothing for their educated sons to do, they are ignorant of the opportunities awaiting the properly educated Negro men, or else they are using such arguments just as an excuse to continue working their boys and garnering the fruits of their labor for their own selfish purposes.

They are educating their girls to enter into lives of unhappiness. If you educate five girls to each boy – who are four of these girls to marry to make for a happy and blissful married life? For that is one of woman's highest ideals.

The other four must accept one of those boys with a handsome face, apparently pleasing manners as well, who has spent all or nearly all of his money for fine clothes with nothing in his head.

A woman, to be matrimonially happy, must have in a husband one whom she can look up to and adore – and it is an impossibility for an educated woman to look up to and adore ignorance.

A man may marry a woman who is well meaning and aspiring that is far below him in intelligence. He has a chance to pull her up to or toward his intellectual level. But an intelligent woman can never pull an ignorant man up to her level. On the contrary, nine times out of 10, he will drag her down to his level, and more especially socially.

Let's look at the work of two nationally known Negro educators – one male, the other female – namely Booker T. Washington and Mary McLeod Bethune. Both established and developed schools of national repute – Mary McLeod Bethune, a school for girls, and Booker T. Washington, a school for both boys and girls.

Now there is no question but that Mary McLeod Bethune did not work as hard in the work of developing womanhood as did Booker T. Washington in developing both man and womanhood.

Both had the assistance, encouragement and endorsement of the white South, as well as the white and philanthropic North, and the support of the colored South. And while Mary McLeod Bethune worked just as hard and earnestly as did Booker T. Washington, has she produced any woman who might truly be called Mary McLeod Bethune the Second? Has she been able to send out into the world any women who have established schools that might justly be called Juniors of their Alma Mater?

On the other hand, we find scattered throughout the Southland scores of schools founded on the Tuskegee plan by men who are graduates and disciples of Tuskegee, who might proudly and justly be dubbed Booker T. Washingtons the second, heading schools that are really junior Tuskegees.

Now there is a natural reason for this. In the study of anatomy and physiology, we find that the average weight of the brains in men is heavier by more than four ounces than that of women, and of course men are capable of doing more work depending upon brain substance than women. It must be, therefore, that the Creator intended that man was to be the leader or else both would have been created with average equal brains.

Very probably there are women who graduated from the Mary McLeod Bethune school who were qualified and prepared to go out into the world and emulate the work of Mary McLeod Bethune. But alas, they married the wrong ignorant man on his appearance and, as a result, the energies and work spent in preparing and educating them for lives of usefulness were blighted. While, when Booker T. Washington graduates married the right thinking and willing to help and do right woman, he was just fortifying himself to do creditable work for racial development. The educated man has five educated women from whom to select a wife, while the educated woman has just one-fifth of one man to select from. The New Negro will be quite different in his educational efforts. In the education of his children, he will not spend the greater part of time and energies in educating his girls to the almost total neglect of the education of the boys. After reviewing the past history of races, both ancient and modern, he will realize even better than I do that the continual development of the Negro people will depend upon the education and development of Negro men of intellectual ability, hence he will, when he has sons who show promise of intellectual ability in any particular line of work, center his energies in providing facilities for the proper development of such qualities. He will also do the same things when able for the proper development of his girls who possessed qualities which, when properly developed, will rebound to strong and useful womanhood.

With the educational efforts that will be practiced by the New Negro in the education of his children, will be the development of Negro men of ability in all walks of Negro life. Then the church heads and leaders will not be up a tree when it comes to supplying intelligent preachers for their congregations, neither will so many of our people suffer and die for want of proper and efficient medical and dental service, as is the case today.

The New Negro doctors will not crowd the cities as second-rate men when their services are needed in the smaller towns and rural districts, where they can be first-rate men and at the same time make adequate money to live like princes – giving their services to people who will highly appreciate and pay for such services.

VII

The New Negro Preacher

The New Negro preacher will, of all things, be a strictly moral gentleman and a strictly businessman.

He will conduct his church and all affairs pertaining to his church work on strictly business principles. In fact, the New Negro preacher will not only be educated in theology and the tenets of his church, but will also have a business and managerial education. Let us follow the course or life's work of one of these New Negro preachers, when he is called to the pastorate of a church.

As a businessman, the first thing he will do will be to get his congregation together and settle the salary question, with an understanding and agreement as to the amount of salary he is to receive, and how and when it is to be paid.

Then he can and will arrange his living expenses accordingly. The salary question being settled satisfactorily, he will not have to and will not be dipping into the treasury of the different auxiliary organizations of the church at will, drawing out funds for which he will never give any account. You will see later that each one who handles or is any way responsible for the church funds will be held strictly accountable for such funds. In fact, the New Negro preacher will be and will act as a kind guardian of those handling the church's monies. He will be as much interested in the financial success of the church as will be its members and friends who donate and contribute their money to the church and its auxiliary organizations. These things all settled and made clear and plain to the members and friends, he will proceed to organize the church on a strictly business basis – by having elected to the boards of deacons, trustees, stewards or such other bodies that are to have in-hand the business management of the church.

Here, in particular, will the New Negro preacher differ from the Old Negro preacher. Instead of picking out a board of "yes" men and women who will do his biddings without question, a board that he can dominate at will, the New Negro preacher will select from his congregation the best business men and women that his congregation affords, and delegate to them the task of directing the business affairs of the church according to their best judgment together with his counsel and advice, when such counsel and advice are thought best by such boards.

Next, he will have the secretary and treasurer and any others who are in any way responsible for the safeguarding of the church's funds, put under sufficient bonds to guarantee the safe and honest handling of the church's money that may pass through their hands.

The New Negro preacher will readily know that millions of the people's money, in the past, have never been accounted for after being put into the hands of some of the most pious members, being left there trusted to their honesty and Christian piety.

Once each year, he will have the books and accounts of all of those in any way responsible for the safeguarding of the church's funds audited by a certified accountant, and any shortage will be made good by the bonding company. That will leave those short in their accounts to deal with the bonding company, and should one occasionally be sent to jail, it would be the bonding company sending him or her to prison and not his or her church brethren and sisters sending him or her there.

The New Negro preacher looking back over past experiences of the church in attempting to erect new churches, repairing and remodeling churches, and after considering the millions of dollars that have been raised for these purposes – as we all well know, enough money to have built temples of worship in the cities and decent churches in the rural districts and smaller towns.

I have, for over 60 years, been donating money to the building funds of Negro churches, and I have yet to see one Negro church, not connected with some white organization, finished and out of debt with money in its treasury to care for the sick and needy.

This being one of the principal duties of the church according to the discipline is caring for the sick and needy, and the burial of the dead of the needy who leave nothing that can be used for burial purposes.

I have seen scores of instances where persons who had been church followers all of their lives, and who contributed regularly to the church when their circumstances permitted, have failed to be supported adequately by the church. I have seen their relatives and friends begging in the streets to raise money for their burial when they died, while the church people sat idly by and the church contributing nothing to their burial funds.

The New Negro preacher will use some of the advanced ideas of the day when he desires to build, remodel or repair his church. One of the principal ideas will be, after safeguarding the church's funds as above stated, to raise enough money to build the church to within the reach of the church's credit. Then he will put the church under the manager form of government. Something on the order of the city manager form of government as is used by most of the progressive cities of the land today, employing as manager some astute businessman of unquestioned honesty and integrity to have sole charge of the construction work to be done. By the time these New Negro ideas prevail there will be men in the race fully qualified for such positions, giving him full charge and responsibility (after he has been put under sufficient bond) of such work as is to be done.

This will leave the church's officers and congregation free to devote their time to the rallying to the church's funds. Under this arrangement, it will be found that the general public will donate more freely to the church, because they will know that what they give will be used for the purposes for which it is given, and not be squandered and stolen as has been and is being done even to this day. There are lots of people today, who are amply able to give to the church, who absolutely refuse to give anything – because they well know from past experience that a very small percentage of what they give is ever used for the purposes for which it is given. Of course, this is not true in all cases, but is true in a very large majority of Negro churches.

There must and will be a revolution in Negro church management, under the New Negro preachers backed up by the New Negro congregations that will in some future day (which I trust is not far distant) will be in the majority not only in the church but all walks of life among the Negroes.

Then the church, under this new regime, will be conducted according to the discipline of the church – which in certain parts will be revised to conform to and meet the ideas of the New Negro congregations.

The New Negro preacher, having all of the above things settled and in operation, will be able to give more of his time to the studying of the Scriptures and preaching the Gospel to his people, and also to giving more of his time to the visitation and administering to the sick and needy, and doing charity work among his parishioners. In short, he will be the true minister. He will not have to spend one-fourth to one-third of the service hours in begging for money, thus killing and making his congregation forget the good that was intended for them in the services.

The New Negro congregation, being intelligent and appreciative of the good work and business management of the New Negro preacher in the affairs of the church, will require but a short while for them to give what they have to give, knowing the church's need and their obligations to the church. They will give freely and quickly of what they will regularly lay aside as church money. When the general collection is taken, there will be no more collections taken for "this, that and the other" as there will be money set aide from the general collection to take care of "this, that and the other." Then the congregation after having heard good services will soon be dismissed to go their way and meditate over the good things they have heard in the services.

The New Negro preacher will fully realize that so long as the church reaches and exerts its influences for good over a small minority of the young people, the men and women of tomorrow, that the church is a miserable and disastrous failure.

His energies and efforts will therefore be centered and exerted to the work of bringing these men and women of tomorrow into the folds of the church. When the Church, the Sunday School and other auxiliary organizations of the Church reach the point in their activities where they can exert an influence of good upon a majority of these men and women of tomorrow, then and not until then will the Church be filling its mission and looked upon by all as a success in its work for the Master.

VIII

The New Negro and His Dead

The New Negro will look upon his dead and their burial in an altogether different light to what the Old Negro looks upon such matters. The New Negro, being endowed with plenty of common sense, will direct his energies toward doing for and making happy his people while they are living; and not as is the case with the Old Negro, neglecting and not properly providing for them – thus tending to make self happy during their loved ones living days, and then when the loved one die, trying to make up for their short coming by spending money lavishly upon them after they are dead.

The Old Negro has carried the burial of their dead to a foolish and extravagant extreme, trying not only to keep up with the Joneses, but in trying to outdo the Joneses.

Men who have spent as much or more on other women than on their wives, and women who have not lived true to their husbands, will when their wife or husband dies and their conscience begins to prick them. They try to make up for their years of delinquency all at one time by spending all the insurance money on them, or else by incurring all the debts they can in providing an elaborate funeral, thus showing to the world how dearly they loved them and how sorely they miss them. Many a family has gone bankrupt in this very way.

The New Negro will be as I have said, endowed with plenty of common sense and will be strictly family people. When a man marries a woman, he will, as he vows at the wedding altar, forsake all others solely for her and will devote his life to provide for making her life happy. The New Negro woman will be the true wife, forsaking all others even until death, devoting her life to the task of making their home one of happiness. She will be the true and model wife and company keeper.

The New Negro will carry insurance, not solely for burial purposes, but more for the purpose of providing the care of the loved ones left behind. The New Negro will too well know that when one of his loved ones is dead that there is nothing more that he can do that will in any way contribute to their happiness, pleasure or comfort – having done all in his power to contribute to their happiness, pleasure and comfort while they were living. He will proceed at the very earliest time to put them away decently, not gorgeously. He, having treated them right when they were living, will have no conscience pricks that he feels that he must atone for by foolhardy extravagance, making a big show to the world. So instead of holding for days, weeks and sometimes more than a month to get the stage set for a big funeral, sometimes even rehearsing for the big show, he will – at the earliest time compatible with circumstances – put them away without display and show of grandeur.

I have known persons to be ill for weeks and months with relatives at distances away who never came near them or contributed one cent toward their comfort and ease. Yet, when such persons die, their relatives who are responsible for their internment will hold their bodies for weeks awaiting the arrival of these trifling distantly located relatives so that they can see their bodies for the last time – false sentiments. The New Negro will down such false sentiments and proceed to bury his dead when they die. When a person is dead, sentiment will not affect him in any way, as his body is then in a state of readiness to return to the clay from whence it came. Then why not return it to the clay from whence it came and be over with it?

The Negro is too sentimental in matters pertaining to death. The New Negro will look upon death in a reasonable and philosophical manner, knowing that death is inevitable to all of us. He will be prepared to, when it comes into his family, stand the ordeal in a sensible, and not in a sentimental, way.

What Is Death?

Death is just a change where one puts off mortality and enters a state of immortality. Among the sweet legends of the past, we read of two islands situated in an unknown sea. The one is called the Island of the Living, the other, the Island of the Dead. The change of abode from the one of these islands to the other is what we call death. Death is just a change. The falling of the leaves is death. The changing of the seasons is death. The wilting of the rose is death. The setting of the sun is death. The ever-going-on changes that surround us daily is death. The taking away of our loved ones is death. Then:

> "Why should we moan departed friends,
> Or shake at death's alarm?
> 'Tis but the voice the Jesus sends
> To call them to his arm."

As the laborer lays down his tools when his day's work is over and returns to his home for a night's rest, so do the inhabitants of that Island of the Living. When life's battle is ended, they lay off the form of morality to put on the form of immorality and embark in their canoes for the other island, that of the dead – "where the wicked shall cease from troubling and the weary shall be forever at rest."

The New Negro, when the grim reaper enters his home, will without days and weeks of prepared splendor and éclat, simply bury his dead because he will well know that if he has not done for them during their living days that what he does in the way of show and splendor after they are gone is simply money wasted in trying to make false impressions on the living world.

IX

The New Negro and Fraternal Organizations

There is something in the mysticisms of fraternal organizations that seems to appeal especially to the Negro. This same something will appeal to the New Negro, who will be strong for fraternal organization also.

When the New Negro reviews the past history and experiences of the Negroes in these organizations, when he recounts the millions of Negro dollars that have been dissipated and stolen in these organizations, when he reviews how certain individuals who headed and controlled these organizations in such a way as to perpetuate the keeping of themselves in control of these organizations, and when he reviews how these certain individuals or rings have controlled and so manipulated the finances of these organizations in such a way that the "Big Fish" continually "ate up the little fish," the New Negro will first consider these organizations from a strictly business standpoint, and will proceed to the task first of putting these organizations on a strictly business basis.

He will no longer trust to a brother's oath and obligation to the organization to keep a brother or sister honest and straight in the handling of the financial affairs of such organizations.

The New Negro will see to it that every officer to whom is trusted the handling of the monies of such organization will be put under good and sufficient bonds in some reliable bonding company in an amount that is sufficient to cover the amount of money to be handled by such members during their term of office or until such time as the organization may order the books and accounts of such officers audited by some public certified accountant or auditor, one whose honesty and veracity is beyond question.

Any shortage found in any officer's accounts will be made good by the bonding company, and the amount of shortage will be a matter between such short member and the bonding company. As previously stated, should a brother occasionally be sent to prison, he would have been sent there by the bonding company and not by his brethren whose obligations are not to send a brother to prison.

This will be the course that the New Negro will adopt in putting the fraternal organizations on a sound business basis. There has been enough of Negroes' money squandered, dissipated and stolen from fraternal organizations in this country to have built and equipped a railroad system.

Another thing that the New Negro will do is to put that branch of such organizations known as death benefit or insurance feature of such organizations on a strictly insurance basis, which will provide ample funds to pay death claims to widows and orphans when it is due. They will not perform as some I know of that are issuing $500 policies to their members payable one-fourth of face value if death occurs during the first year, one-half if death occurs during the second year, three-fourths if death occurs during the third year, and full face value of policy after the policy has been in force for three full years – charging some of them 25 cents per month and some 50 cents per month as premiums. Think of it. A person would have to be in such an organization for 83 and two-thirds years to put $500 into the death funds. Now if no one lives long enough to put the amount that his policy calls for in the death funds, and the organization is not investing the death funds into some profitable business, then pray and tell me where is the money coming from to pay these death claims after a few years when the older heads begin dying out?

The New Negro will not go into these organizations under such terms and management, and these organizations in order to survive, and my guess is that they always will survive, will have to adopt a strictly business management in all of their departments and ramifications.

The Old Negro was too trustful. When he was obligated into one of these organizations and after considering the severity and stringency of the oath he had taken, he just could not see how a brother under such obligations could go wrong. He trusted all to the strong obligations that his brethren who were officers had taken. He did not further trouble himself to inquire or investigate in any way of the financial affairs of his lodge, believing that his brethren who had taken the same stringent obligations that he himself had taken could not steal.

The New Negro will be educated or partially educated at least and will be inquisitive regarding the money affairs of his organization or lodge. It will be no longer possible for a ruling ring of officials to bring in false reports of the financial affairs of the order winning the plaudits of the masses, sending the delegates homeward bound with glowing reports of the successful strides the order is making.

The only way for the heads of these organizations to perpetuate or keep themselves in office will be that of strict honesty together with good business management – thereby proving themselves as leaders and businessmen worthy of being followed, and capable of continuing to enthuse new life and new ideas into the organization and handling tasks regarding finances of the order to the best, safest and most profitable advantages of the order. Then, and not until then, will we see some good Grand Lodge building finished and out of debt, also many of the halls and lodge rooms more than mere shells with a roof over them. Under the guidance of the New Negro, the building of a Grand Lodge Temple or even the building of a local hall and lodge room will be a strictly business undertaking.

The New Negro will not, with a few hundred dollars, start the building of a $2,000 hall and lodge room – or with a few thousand dollars in cash, begin the erection of a $60,000 Grand Temple – with no ideas as to how or where the balance is to be raised. On the contrary, he will, first of all, raise enough funds to carry the erection of the building to within the reach of the organizations credit. In this way, they will not undertake the erection of more expensive buildings than are really needed.

Then under some one as a manager and builder, who will be bonded, will be entrusted the erection of such building. Under this plan, when a building is once started, with the cash on hand and the amount of credit the order is good for, the building can be carried on to full completion.

To some, this may seem a long time before an order can be in a financial condition to start and complete the erection of a building. Not so long a time as some would think. For once these organizations are put on a strictly sound business basis, with the stealing and squandering of its funds stopped, their membership would increase so rapidly that in a surprisingly short time they would find their treasuries filling at an almost unbelievable rate. One of the reasons being, there are hundreds of thousands of thinking people of today that have quit these organizations because of their dissatisfactions with the present management of these organizations, and such thinkers would gladly and willingly not only return themselves but would bring their sons and daughters into these organizations.

Under this new order of things, the fraternal organizations will become giants in the financial world. These organizations will use their surplus monies for the erection of decent office and business buildings that will be a continuous source of revenue for their treasuries.

When they once reach this stage of development and advancement, they will realize that their members will be more punctual in the payment of their dues. And, one will not find nearly one-half of the adult population to be ex-members of some fraternal organization that at one time apparently flourished, only to finally land on the rocks stranded with a depleted treasury and thousands of dollars of unpaid death claims due to the widows and orphans of those who had passed on. The organization had been bled to the last drop by that official ring that manipulated the financial affairs of these organizations.

These organizations will, with their surplus monies, also go into other profitable enterprises that will give employment to the younger people of the race.

In fact, with the honest handling and safe investing of such monies, it will be through the fraternal organizations that the New Negro will enter the field of big business.

I do not want to be understood to mean that this will be the only avenue through which the New Negro will find his way into big business. But this is just an example of one of the many ways, and especially in the cooperative business.

Of course among the New Negroes will be found many individuals who, by their own efforts together with good judgment and good business tact, will become financial giants.

The Grand Heads of these fraternal organizations under the control of the New Negroes will be much more discreet in the granting of dispensations for the making of new members at "bargain day prices" than did the Old Negro Hand Heads who granted them so that they (the Grand Heads) could get so much per head for each one who accepted these "bargain day prices" regardless of the fitness of such candidates for membership.

The New Negro Grand Heads will not do this, for in the first place their business sense will cause them to accept such positions only at a salary that is commensurate the with the work to be done. It will be a salary that will be sufficient to care for his need during the term of office. So you can see that they will not have to resort to the "bargain day" and other tactics to raise sufficient revenue to pay them for their services during their terms in office.

The old custom of granting dispensations, thereby getting large classes of candidates and then going through the whole ritual ceremony of initiation in one night, will be abandoned by the New

Negro Grand heads. They will well know that people initiated into the order in such manner will not understand the real meaning of the oath they take or the fundamental principles of the order, hence do not make good and devoted members. Then too, it just fills the lodges with people who are undesirable as members, people whom decent self-respecting people do not care to be seen in the company with in public parades or gatherings. This practice also fills the lodges with the unhealthy, thereby increasing the death and sick rate in the lodges.

These New Negro Grand Heads will allow members to come into the orders according to the ritualistic rules and regulations of their orders, and being initiated in strict conformity to the ritual given in one night or session only so much as is provided for in the ritual, making such inductions into the orders just as impressive and solemn as possible. They will do this so that when one is fully initiated into the order, he will fully understand the obligations he has taken, also understand his duties to the order and the fundamental principles of the order.

When these organizations are conducted in this manner, the Grand Heads and officers of these organizations – as well as the heads and officers of the subordinate lodges – can, at the beginning of their term of office, calculate very closely the amount of revenue that will be taken in during such term because their membership will be composed of dependable and reliable members. Thus, they will be in position of governing the terms of spending in each department accordingly. They will also be able to govern the rates of benefits according to the rates of income of such departments, such as insurance and sick and accident benefits.

When the world sees and is convinced that these organizations are being run and conducted on a strictly safe business basis, people will willingly come into them paying the regular initiation fees, thus doing away with necessity of dispensations and "bargain day" fees in order to get new members. They will come in paying the regular initiation fees, which in some cases will be as much as the fees paid by four or five "bargain day" members. The insurance and sick and accident risks would be from three-fourths to four-fifths less than it would be on the four or five "bargain day" members. The order would be more dependable, reliable and permanent – with members whose dues could be counted upon for years to come. Members taken in, in strict conformity to the laws laid down in regard to health, moral standing and reputation for sobriety and faithfulness. Members of whom the order might well be proud.

When these New Negro leaders restore these fraternal organizations to this high standard of perfection and rid the orders of the greater part of the riffraff brought into them through the "bargain day" rackets, then will the world look upon and respect the Negro fraternal organizations as being organizations that decent and right thinking people would be proud to be a member.

Then, good people would not be ashamed to turn out in parade or celebration of the order, but to the contrary would be proud to be seen in such company so that the world would know that they belonged to such an honorable band of brethren.

X

The New Negro in Agriculture

The Negro by nature seems to be adapted to tilling the soil. He seems to take naturally to agriculture. The New Negro will not be different in nature to his fore parents in this respect, and with the knowledge he will gain from the agricultural and mechanical state colleges, the many pamphlets and circulars sent out free for the asking from the Department of Agriculture of the national government, and the daily radio programs of the home and farm hour nationally broadcasted at noon each weekday during the noon hour – and with the good work the government is doing with the CCC in soil conservation, which the New Negro will learn.

The New Negro farmer will be a much more successful farmer than were his ancestors. He will learn to make two, yea three, blades of grass grow where his ancestors only made one blade of grass grow, and often none at all.

Being able to do this, the New Negro will not need to buy 100 or more acres of land in order to have enough on which to make a decent living. On the contrary, he will buy and own only a small acreage, and with the advanced knowledge in agriculture and soil conservation, on these few acres in diversified crops he will make an independent living for himself and family. With the radio, the automobiles and good roads, he will be able to cope with his city brother in affairs social, educational, style and what not. With the preparations going on now for rural electrification, he will have all of the modern conveniences at his finger tips that his city brothers now enjoy.

These sturdy, substantial and reliable farmer citizens will be a great asset of the race and one of the dependable sources of recruiting the New Negro citizens who will become the leaders of the New Negro ideas and doings.

I say this because the majority of the Negroes in this country are rural inhabitants, and as I see it, will remain rural inhabitants. So one can readily see that if the Negro race is ever to reach the stage of development where the New Negro ideas are to prevail among the majority of all the Negroes in this country, then the majority of those with New Negro ideas and ideals must come from the rural districts.

You, dear reader, may think that time when the New Negro ideas will prevail a long way off. So it may be, but you must remember that it has taken a long time – since the 1860s to the 1940s – to almost completely eliminate the Negroes from full political freedom and to kill the Negroes' interest in government and good citizenship. They are on the fence listening to the siren plea of the communists, the socialists, the reds, etc.

That is one of the things that prompted the attempt of writing this book. I want to get my people back into the folds of good citizenship and back into and a part of this good old democratic form of government of ours. Then we can call on our government and not on the other man's government. I want my people to have a claim on this government by virtue of being full-fledged citizens of the government, thereby making themselves a part of the government and not merely native residents of our government. Do you realize that 90% of the Negro population of this country are not good bona-fide full-fledged citizens? They do not seem to realize that the further they get away from good government, the more they become restricted in their liberties and rights.

I am not advocating that the Negroes get back into the government solely for the purpose of voting. As for voting, I shall attempt later to show that, with the conditions of political affairs in this country at the present time, it is better that the 90% of Negroes are out of politics. I shall attempt to show later that Negroes being out of politics is just hastening the day when the New Negro will be welcomed back into the political affairs of the country and that he will return there to be a permanent fixture in the nation's politics.

The New Negro farmer will be known as the concentrated farmer because he will concentrate his farming activities on small farms, getting all that is to be had from such small areas – thereby cutting to the bone all such expenses as help, fertilizers and rental costs when he has to rent the land which he tills – also cutting to a minimum the animal or mechanical power needed in the farming process.

With the interest that the national, state and county governments are beginning to take in education of the rural Negro youth, it will only be necessary for the rural boy or girl to go away from home to receive a college or professional education. The high school and vocational guidance school will take care of their other needs.

The New Negro farmer will be like the other New Negroes, saving and judicious in their spending, always laying away a part of their earnings for a rainy day. He will rear his family with the ideas of economy, thrift and usefulness not only on themselves but usefulness to others as well. These things he will deeply impress upon them. He will also raise up his children enthusiastically imbued with the ideal of good citizenship deeply instilled not only into their minds, it will also permeate their very beings.

Sixteen or 18 years ago, there was a great exodus of the Southern Negroes to the North and West. Today, the tide seems to have turned, and the Negroes are gradually returning to the Southland. Why? Because, after all, they are realizing that the Southern white man is the right meaning and right doing Negroes' best friend.

When the New Negroes come in the majority of the Negro race, the New Negro and right thinking and well-meaning Southern white man will get together and work out the racial problem to satisfaction of both the Caucasian and Negro races. They are the only ones who ever can, or will, solve the race problems to the satisfaction of all concerned.

The New Negro will be as opposed to social equality, or I would rather say social intercourse of the two races, as will be the Caucasians. The New Negroes will set their own social standards, whether or not they will be patterned after the white man's social standards I am not able to say and I will not attempt to guess. I will await and let the New Negro set those standards to meet the requirements and needs of the New Negro people.

The New Negro will not put his money into or support those organizations of national repute that purport to be great exponents of Negro rights in this country when, in reality, by their actual workings they are really creating (away down in the Negro's heart) an antagonistic feeling towards the government of the country – just making more fertile the fields for the production of a sentiment favorable to the pleas and doctrines being preached to the people by the communist, the socialist, the radical, the reds, etc.

It is true that these organizations, in some isolated instances, do good work in vindicating the rights of some individual. Just remember that in doing so, the adverse publicity given the case, especially through the Negro press, drives tens of thousands of Negroes just a little further from the ideas of respect for good government by creating in them an antagonism to the government of the land. They there create a nucleus for some of these anti-democratic forms of government organizations to work upon.

Now I ask you dear reader, in all fairness and without prejudice, when one of these organizations vindicates the rights of one individual and in so doing drives tens of thousands of Negroes just a little further from the respect of good government and just a little nearer to communism, socialism or some other form of anti-government "isms," have they done the race more good than they have harm?

The only way in which the Negro is to obtain his rights in this country is for the Negro to qualify himself as a full-fledged citizen (and ever remain so qualified) of this government. Now, I do not mean that if one individual Negro so qualifies himself that in so doing that he will be individually able to demand and obtain his rights. What I mean in saying this is that the Negroes as a race must qualify themselves and ever remain qualified as full-fledged citizens; and that they not only keep themselves so qualified, but must bring their children up with the same ideas and principles so drilled into them that it is a civic duty to qualify themselves as full-fledged citizens so that they in turn will feel it a civic duty to do the same thing for their children – a kind of "endless chain" affair growing stronger and stronger with the coming of each succeeding generation.

This process must go on over a period of years before the Negro will be regarded and looked upon as a full-fledged citizen and entitled to the rights of all good citizens.

Just as it has taken years to get the ideas of good citizenship and the support of good government out of the Negro's head, it will take years to get the Negro back to good citizenship and loyal and faithful supporters of good government.

If the Negro is ever to fight for his rights in the government, he must do his fighting within the government. And, in order to make his fight within the government, he must, himself, get into and make himself a part of the government and not depend upon putting his money in some organization in some afar away Northern city, expecting such organization to be successful in obtaining for the Negro, away down here in Dixie, his rights and justices.

The sooner the Negro learns to quit putting his money to such organizations, and get himself into the government by qualifying and making himself a part of the government, the sooner will he find himself being respected as a good citizens and a real part of the government.

If these organizations had spent the money that they have taken out of the Southern Negroes' pockets in educating and building up among the Negroes of the South a sentiment that would have brought the Southern Negroes into government as good, true, faithful and loyal citizens, then a larger part of the cases on which they have spent thousands of dollars in vindicating the rights of some individual would never have happened.

XI

The New Negro and the Negro Press

The New Negro newspaper will be a potent power for good, in advocating and using its influence in bringing and keeping the Negro close to government.

It will not be a sensational and yellow sheet, as are some of the leading colored newspapers of today – hunting and seeking some scandal involving some prominent Negro. Such stuff will find no place in the New Negro newspaper.

Have you ever read one of these "yellow scandal sheets" through, and found one sentence in it advising and encouraging its readers to get closer to or within the government by qualifying themselves as true and loyal citizens of the government? The whole tone and trend of their articles are calculated to alienate or draw the Negro away from citizenship and good government.

They always show up the bad side of a case where whites and Negroes are involved, holding the Negro up as injured innocence. It is true that the Negro generally gets the worst of it in a case where he is involved with a white person.

I am not implying that the Negro is always in the right, and that the treatment that he receives is not always just. These yellow scandal sheets always claim injustice for the Negro; although in most cases the happenings are hundreds, and often times thousands, of miles away from where these sheets are published and the publishers have no way of verifying the articles which they publish to the world as facts. They just publish what is sent in oftentimes by some biased, irresponsible, prejudiced person. They, without verification, go ahead and publish it to the world just so long as it makes interesting reading, and is showing the Negro up as injured innocence.

Most or nearly all of the present day Negro newspapers are great advocates of those organizations that purport to be great exponents of Negro rights in this country. When one of these organizations takes up one of these cases to vindicate some individual's rights, then we get the big red headlines in these yellow scandal sheets.

Where there comes about a scandal involving some prominent Negro or Negress, we again get the big red headlines and oftentimes pictures of the party or parties involved.

I ask, is this kind of journalism doing the race any good? And I answer, no, a thousand times no. I will further say they are leading the race to the point where socialism, communism or any of the other kinds of "isms" opposed to the democratic form of our government will get an attentive ear from the average Negro. It is very evident that the majority of the present day Negro newspapers (not all) are really doing the average Negro more harm than good because they are getting the average Negro farther and farther away from good citizenship and respect for our government.

Financially, some of these "yellow scandal sheets" are a success. I have a very poor opinion of one who will lead the greater part of a race away from good government, making of them fit subjects to be preyed upon by the siren pleadings of some anti-good democratic form of government organizations just for the few paltry dollars that they are garnering for their own selfish uses.

This country is filled with foreigners who are preaching the doctrines of these anti-government organizations to the American people, who in large numbers are falling for it. Now is the time the Negro press ought to be extolling the Negroes of this country to get closer and into this good old democratic form of government of ours.

Instead, they are publishing articles that are creating, away deep down in the Negroes' hearts, a feeling of antagonism to the government of the land.

This feeling makes the Negro lax and opposed to giving evidence or information to the authorities that would lead to the apprehension and punishment of criminals.

I see it this way, if one is a criminal, that person (white or black) ought to be apprehended and punished regardless of color, race or nativity. This fact ought to be impressed continually on the average Negro's mind.

Of all the races in this country, the Negro ought to be the nearest to good government; because, as you know, his color is against him and he needs the protection of the government more so than any other race of people in this country. The Negro cannot reasonably expect the full protection of the law, when instead of being a part of the government as a good citizen, he has a feeling of antagonism deep down in his heart against the legal instituted authorities of the law.

While the Negro does not always get justice at the hand of the legal instituted authorities, he should get himself into the government by qualifying himself as a citizen and a part of the government. When he shall have done this, and brings his children up with this sprit and aim in their breasts, he will have made a long stride towards obtaining justice for the Negroes in this country.

Show to the world that the Negro is as faithful and loyal to good government as is the white man. The New Negro newspaper will be such a different sheet from the present day popular "yellow scandal sheets." The New Negro Press is different in every way. It will be a strong advocate and exponent of good government. The tenor and tone of its editorials will be strongly advocating good government and good citizenship. Ever keeping its readers and especially the young people of the race – the men and women of tomorrow – reminded of the duties and importance of good citizenship.

It will literally drill the ideas of good citizenship into the minds of its readers. Instead of scandal, it will print news of people who are doing something worthwhile, as an encouragement to the younger people. It will be a mechanism that will stimulate their ambitions and desires to do something themselves that will be worthy of note.

The New Negro will be strong in fiction writing. Writing books that will, by their very tone and subject matter, be uplifting and inspiring to the younger people – ever bringing and keeping before them the importance of good citizenship.

There will be published by the New Negro editors monthly journals or magazines that will readily take on a national aspect. These are journals that every New Negro will be proud to have in his home for himself and family to read. The trend of the major part of the articles in these journals will be to bring and keep the Negro closer to good government. And as we see the New Negro literature grown in favor with the reading public, just so will we see the wane of the popularity of the yellow scandal sheets. The "yellow scandal sheets" are doomed to go.

As the New Negro becomes more enlightened and more numerous, and gets nearer to good government, he will soon begin to realize that the yellow scandal sheets are doing the race as a whole more harm than good.

The New Negro will not only not read these "yellow scandal sheets" himself, but not allow them in his home and will, in every way he can, discourage his children from reading them. He will do this because he will fully realize that these sheets are acting as direct deterrents to real substantial racial progress in the right direction. Hence, the "yellow scandal sheets" will pass on and become just a matter of history in the doings and struggles of the American Negro – a history of which the New Negro will be very much ashamed.

XII

The New Negro in Politics

In the preceding pages I have been attempting through the New Negro, whom I have tried to portray, to show some of the requisites for the Negro's permanent entry into the politics of the country.

In this the concluding chapter, I shall attempt to show how and when, and under what condition, this New Negro will come permanently into the politics of this country.

First of all, I will say that, along with the development of this New Negro, there will also be a development of a new white man. For the sake of brevity, I shall refer to this new Caucasian man as "Young America." This "Young America" will be a great big fellow, not particularly in stature but a big fellow in his liberal way of thinking and dealing with his fellow-man, big in his ideas and ideals in political affairs – which will be of the broad democratic type.

He will be too big to be bound by political parties and politicians who in turn take their orders and abide by the dictates of the monied and cooperated interests, who would dictate as to how and for whom this "Young America" must cast their ballots.

"Young America" will have no party obligations and will not allow himself to be tied by any parties or politicians as is the case today with the white electorate. He will rebel against the cooperated interests and money powers controlling the elections of the country through a coterie of astute politicians.

This "Young America," the men and women of tomorrow, will be thinkers for themselves and this will mean the downfall of the old political parties that are dominated today by the monied interests of the country and their henchmen, the politicians.

Just as sure as I am writing this, in a surprisingly short time the old political parties will have passed on, or else this country will be strife ridden with socialism, communism, radicalism or some other kind of "ism" opposed to the democratic form of government as laid down in the Constitution – which provides that this is to be a government of the people, for the people and by the people, and each citizen is given one vote in electing the officials whose business is to run the government for the best interests of the majority of the citizens of this country.

Take a perspective view of the trend of politics of the present time, and it is alarming to see what an attentive ear these organizations, which are opposed to the democratic form of government, are getting from our American population. Of course, they will never get strong enough to gain control of our government. At the rate they are gaining, in some future day they will cause the American people to fuse the old political parties into one party in order to be able to save our constitutional form of government and this will be the beginning of the demise of these old political parties.

This fusion of the old political parties will be necessary because of the tremendous strength these anti-democratic form of government organizations will grow to such an extent within a generation or two, that the fusion of the old political parties, the upholders of constitutional form of government, will be necessary to outvote these other organizations. They will become so strong that the division of the upholders of democratic form of government by two separate parties fighting each other for the control of the government will allow these organizations to unite their forces and gain control of the government. Hence the fusion of the two. Our national leaders will foresee these dangers and before it is too late, bring the American public to a realization of the peril threatening our government, and will convince the American electorate of the necessity of forgetting party ties and affiliations and unite into one solid front for the purpose of saving the Constitution and defeating these anti-constitutional organizations in their efforts to gain control of this government.

This will for a time seem safe, but the monied interests and politicians will continue to dominate things political and of course will continue to drive the man in the streets to look favorable on these other organizations and he will continue to join the rank of these other organizations until after a few years when they will again threaten the control of constitutional government.

The millions of white children who are in the schools and colleges today, under the educational systems in practice at the present with these practices and methods of teaching being constantly changed and improved upon, are making of "Young America" free, broad and liberal thinkers, especially in political and governmental affairs. This of course will make them less prejudicial and more liberal in their dealing with the New Negro than are the adult white population of the present time.

This "Young America" when the one party is threatened with defeat, by a combination of these different "isms" which are opposed to our constitutional form of government, for when the old political parties join forces in one party, we may expect to see and will witness the joining of forces of these other "isms" which will so nearly divide the American white man into equal camps that the stage of desperation will have come to save the Constitution of this country. It is here that "Young America" will come to the fore.

By this time, "Young America" will have grown in numbers where they will exert a strong influence on the politics of the day, due to the fact that the present day electorate's lines will be thinned by the grim reaper. "Young America" will bring new ideas and methods into the political practices of the day.

One of these methods will be in the way of nominating candidates for office by primary. Not a primary patterned in any way after the present day primaries, where a nomination in the primary of a candidate to office by a small minority of all the citizens will be equivalent to election.

These primaries will decide who are to be the candidates whose names will appear on the tickets in the general election. The old political parties being dead, those who offer themselves as candidates for election to office will have to take their stand on some definite platform as "Young America" will be only interested in candidates to the extent of the platforms and measures that these candidates stand for.

Not as at the present day where the electorate is interested in what political party the candidate represents. The platforms and measures that these candidates stand for are what will interest "Young America," the personal standing of such candidates as to honesty and reliability, as to whether such candidates will live up to the carrying out of the things that their platforms call for, will receive the electorate's consideration.

In the new primary systems there will be certain requisites for a candidate wishing to get his or her name on the primary ballot and when these requisites are compiled the candidate's name will be put on the ballot for the primary. Thus as many as care to and can comply with the requirements of this law in order to have one's name appear upon the primary ballot can do so, and then go before the voters with their platforms and the measures that they stand for. When this primary is over, the two highest candidates will be entitled to have their names printed on the ballots of the general election in November. These two and no one else's name will be allowed on the ticket for the general election. In this way no one who voted in the primary will be bound by oath to the support of any candidate, thus leaving the whole electorate the privileges of studying the candidates, their platforms and the measures they stand for in deciding on the one for whom they will cast their ballot; then the one who is elected will be selected by a majority of all the citizens of his election area of which such candidate is to represent – be it town, city, country, state or nation. Then such elected candidates will be held accountable to a majority of all the citizens of their respective election areas.

By the time these things are put into practice, these anti-constitutional organizations will have gained such grounds as to about equally divide the white electorate of this country. To save the country from the control of these anti-constitutional forms of government, "Young America" – those broad reasoners, liberal thinkers, unbiased and unprejudiced in their dealing and in their feeling toward their fellow-man regardless to race or color or previous political affiliations – will unite with the New Negro in their efforts to save the government from the control of these anti-governmental organizations.

In all of the wars of this country where the Negro has been drafted into them, the Negro has always acquitted himself with credit and honor and has been a wonderful auxiliary in gaining the day for this government and upholding the honor of the American flag.

There is another war brewing, a war that will effect the very vitals of constitutional government of this country, one that will be of vital importance to every citizen of this country who is a lover of our government as laid down in the Constitution. This war will be a war of ballots between those who are believers in the upholding of our constitutional form of government and those who would destroy our constitutional form of government. A war that will and must be so decisive in its victory as to forever destroy the hopes and aspirations of those who would destroy our government. This will only be done when "Young America" and the New Negro unite in this one common cause.

The one object foremost in the writer's mind in urging the Negro people of all America to get back, and make themselves a part of, this government by qualifying themselves as full-fledged citizens – and teaching and drilling the same ideas into the heads of their children – is that the American Negro will be ready at the clarion call of "Young America."

Some of you may think and say that there is no use in my qualifying myself as these things will never come to pass in my day; but you must remember that you will be helping to lay the solid foundation for the American Negro's permanent entry back into the politics of the country. You should also remember that the political isolation and slavery that the American Negro is now subjected to, is due to the foundation laid by our forefathers in the unwise courses that they took in politics, during and after the days of Reconstruction and carpetbag rule in the South. This, I have tried to portray in the section of this book devoted to the Old Negro.

When these new election methods or their equivalent or better are put into practice in America, where a majority of all of the citizens will elect the officers to run the American government; then will we get some laws enacted and put on the statute books that will be for the benefit of all the people; because they will be put there by lawmakers who were elected to the law-making bodies by a majority of all of the citizens of their respective election areas, and of course they will feel themselves being held accountable to a majority of all the citizens of their election areas, and not as at present held accountable only to the monied interests and their henchmen, the politicians who manipulated them into office with the aid of the monies supplies by the monied interests. Just there to do the biddings of their bosses, the monied interests and politicians.

When one is elected to an office of the national government (Congress, Senate, or even the Presidency), he will have been elected to such office by a majority of all of the citizens, and will not have been manipulated into office by the vested interests and professional politicians by only a minority of all the citizens of his election area. Then these representatives can and will give their time to the enactment of laws that will be beneficial to all of the people. They will not, as at the present time, give a greater part of their time to keeping up political fences at home that our present national representatives have to do. They know that their political life will depend upon their doing something for all of the people.

Owing to the methods that the old political parties are resorting to hold control of the government, they are driving the man in the street to look favorably upon these anti-government organizations. I am pleading with the American Negro to take no part with them and above all do not give an attentive ear to those organizations that would destroy our form of government.

By letting the old political parties continue to drive the man in the street to these organizations against our government, thus strengthening those organizations, they are hastening the day of that great battle of ballots. The Negro by being qualified and ready will come into the fray and join with "Young America" in winning the battle for good democratic form of government. Thus, wrestling from the monied interests and the professional politicians the control of politics and the government and also smashing the hopes and ambitions of those anti-government organizations of gaining control of the government, and also gaining for the American Negro a permanent place in American political life – "killing three birds with one stone."

The new Caucasian men and women who will come in control of the government will not so easily forget the good services that the New Negro will render in assisting in liberating this government from the clutches of the politicians and monied interests and of his assistance in dooming those anti-government organizations. I say that "Young America" will not so easily forget the Negroes' assistance in this battle of ballots as did their ancestors forget the Negroes' services in the past wars. This "Young America" will be too big and broad to stoop to petty prejudices against an enlightened people, as will be the New Negro. This "Young America" will be too broad minded and liberal to forget and scorn the people who fought side by side with them in this battle of ballots for the upholding of constitutional government.

"Young America" will be looking for real men and women and in the New Negro they will find real men and women of character, integrity, intelligence, honesty and security of purposes – real worthwhile men and women who can be depended upon to assist in upholding the principles of our government.

It has taken 70 years for the Southern whites to effectually put the Negro out of politics and kill his interest in government. It is going to take time, I cannot say how long, for the Negro to get back into politics and the government.

I have tried to show how the Negro can regain his place in politics; but the time it will take will to a great extent depend upon the Negro himself, by his qualifying himself as a citizen of the government and not aligning himself with any of the old corrupt political parties of the present day. Instead, he should align himself with men and the measures they stand for. It is better that the Negro is out of the present day, corrupt politics because their present political tactics are just hastening their doom.

When this new era in politics is ushered in by "Young America," the Negro, by steering clear of the present day politics, can enter with clean hands to help save the day for constitutional government, as did those Negro soldiers enter the fray at San Juan Hill in Cuba and help save the day for the American Army in upholding the American flag on that day.

Now, in conclusion: I sincerely implore and beg my people to get back to and into the government by qualifying themselves as full-fledged citizens of our government and to stay so qualified; not to align themselves with either of the old corrupt political parties, let them have the rope and they will soon break their own political necks; and above everything else do not in any way take any part with any of those organizations which would destroy our constitutional form of government. Do these three things for the sake and edification of the present day Negro race and for the laying of a sound basis upon which the millions of present day Negro school children and the millions of pre-school age and unborn Negro children may honorably enter into American politics.

The End

EDITOR'S NOTES

THE AUTHOR
Dr. Thomas Leroy Jefferson Jr.
(1867-1939)

The first Black American doctor to practice in West Palm Beach, the oldest municipality in the country, Dr. Thomas Leroy Jefferson was an 1892 graduate of Meharry Medical College in Nashville (Tennessee) and a native of Hazlehurst (Mississippi). After moving to New Iberia (Louisiana), he worked as a teacher before marrying Georgia Broussard and relocating to Tennessee to attend medical school. After his graduation, the Jeffersons lived in Orange (Texas) before moving to New Orleans (Louisiana), where Maude Kay was born. By 1902, they had settled in Palm Beach (Florida).

Dr. Jefferson was born two years after slavery ended, and always celebrated his ethnicity although his father and one of his sisters chose to live life passing as Caucasians. In Southeast Florida Pioneers: The Palm & Treasure Coasts, William McGoun wrote that Thomas Sr. became a major cotton crower and a leading citizen of Hazlehurst possibly because of a legend that he was related to the America's third president, Thomas Jefferson, through Sally Hemmings.

Seemingly unphased by his darker skin and favored upbringing, Dr. Jefferson remained committed to the African-American community and, soon after arriving in Palm Beach, began practicing medicine in the Styx community. By 1911 and throughout the Great Depression, he worked from an office in a frame building on North Olive Avenue in West Palm Beach. Called the "bicycle doctor," he is described as "a lean, quiet healer" and respected community member with "personality."

It is said that Dr. Jefferson did not have creditors because he "paid cash" for everything, enabling him to keep his property after the 1929 market crash that took everything else. Historians also record that Dr. Jefferson was often

seen peddling around downtown puffing "one of his ever-present cigars," and frequently making rounds on his bike during his 40 years as a physician and owner of a drug store.

He was also well-known for his work treating Native Americans of the Glades tribe. Because of his contributions to the Blacks and Natives in the area, Dr. Jefferson's story has been included among tomes celebrating the history of Florida and Palm Beach alike. In addition to McGoun's work, other books mentioning Dr. Jefferson's life include: The Indian River Settlement: 1842-1849 by Joseph D. Cushman Jr., A History of Riviera Beach, Florida by Lynn Brink, and Incomparable Delray Beach—Its Early Life and Lore by Cecil and Margoann Farrar.

Through his only daughter's marriage to Carl Robinson, Dr. Jefferson's family has grown to include three grandchildren, three great-grandchildren, two great-great-grandchildren, and three great-great-great-grandchildren.

Dr. Jefferson was 70 years old when the world was first gifted with The Old Negro and The New Negro. This was only two years before his demise while having his appendix removed at Pine Ridge Hospital in West Palm Beach. His interment was at Evergreen Cemetery in Palm Beach.

In retrospect, the duration of Dr. Jefferson's life "almost precisely cover the era from Emancipation to the beginning of the modern Civil Rights Movement.

He was a son of slavery and a father of the contemporary African-American, both spiritually and temporally," McGoun eloquently stated.

To pay homage to his indisputable legacy of devotion to heal all communities, the **T. Leroy Jefferson Medical Society** (tljmedicalsociety.org) was established by fellow medical professionals in West Palm Beach in 1947. After being rejuvenated in 1990 by a new wave of young physicians, the organization was incorporated in 1991 and granted 501(c)3 status in 2000. Today, the group adopts schools, hosts medical information luncheons, and conducts health fairs each year to foster healthier Palm Beach communities.

THE EDITOR

Dr. Mary Michelle Jefferson

Also known as Mylia Tiye Mal Jaza, Mary Jefferson is an author who also assists others seeking to publish with copyright, editing and other services via **BePublished.org**. The youngest daughter of Susie Williams Jefferson and George Comas Jefferson Sr., Mary's father is the son of the late Rev. James "Brother" Russell Jefferson (on the back cover) and Jimmie "Sister" Lynch Jefferson—who had seven boys and seven girls in Hazlehurst, MS. It is said that Brother's grandfather, Thomas, one day changed the family's surname from Meeks to Jefferson during the late 18th or early 19th century to honor his lineage as a descendant of Thomas Jefferson and Sally Hemmings (although DNA testing has not proved this shared bloodline). Sister's parents were Tom Lynch and Jimmy Chess Lynch. Brother's parents were James Andrew Jefferson and Ollie Estelle Short Jefferson. Dr. Thomas LeRoy Jefferson was Brother's uncle, making the history-making physician Mary's great-great-uncle.

1880 U.S. Census	
Caroline Roberts (mother)	67
Thomas Jefferson	48
Susan (wife)	41
Ellen (daughter)	20
Henry (son)	18
Caroline (daughter)	15
Thomas (son)	12
Eliabert (daughter)	10
James (son)	6
Idell (son)	4
Joseph (son)	2

Deemed as a "jack of all trades, master of each" and the quintessential professional artist, Mary—a Mississippi native and former Uptown Dallas resident—currently resides in Chicago, IL. She obtained a bachelor's degree from Jackson State University, a master's from the University of Texas at Dallas, and an honorary doctorate from Trinity Evangelical Christian University.

Mary's career history includes having her visual art work exhibited in cities including Dallas and Chicago, establishing a solid journalism career (*The Clarion-Ledger*, *The Dallas Morning News*, WLBT-TV3, WJSU-88.5FM, *The Dallas Examiner*, and *Eclipse Magazine*), modeling and acting for major companies, (Mary Kay, Match.Com and Proctor & Gamble), and operating her own businesses that deliver services ranging from group training and office assistance to charitable work and self-publishing assistance.

One with visions of opening an oxygen bar/tea room and small chain of all-suite and themed hotels, Mary has also been featured on several underground CDs and has her own published EP ("Freedom Found" by Goddess Sage). She also has a host of other books available worldwide—eight books she wrote using the pseudonym "Mylia Tiye Mal Jaza," and she re-released two books that were written by ancestors of hers. Her titles to date are:

AND
Plea For Peace
Seen In Other Words
Elegies of a Goddess
Scientific Evidence God Exists
Life Is Beautiful: La Vita E Bella
Life Is Beautiful: La Vita Es Hermosa
All for Show: Film & Television Scripts
The Facts of Reconstruction by John R. Lynch
The Old Negro and The New Negro by T. LeRoy Jefferson, M.D.

www.ingramcontent.com/pod-product-compliance
Lightning Source LLC
Chambersburg PA
CBHW031233280526
45784CB00004B/1562